BEST OF THE BEST

500 Fast & Fabulous

FIVE ★ STAR

5 INGREDIENT

RECIPES

BEST OF THE BEST
500 Fast & Fabulous
FIVE ★ STAR
5 INGREDIENT
RECIPES

Gwen McKee
and
Barbara Moseley

Illustrated by Tupper England

QUAIL RIDGE PRESS
Preserving America's Food Heritage

Library of Congress Cataloging-in-Publication Data

Best of the best : 500 fast and fabulous 5-star 5-ingredient recipes /
    edited by Gwen McKee and Barbara Moseley ; illustrated by Tupper England.
    — Ring-bound ed.
    p. cm.
        Includes index.
        ISBN-13: 978-1-934193-05-1
        ISBN-10: 1-934193-05-4
1. Quick and easy cookery. 2. Cookery, American. I. McKee, Gwen. II. Moseley, Barbara. III.
    Title: Five hundred fast and fabulous
five-star five-ingredient recipes. IV. Title: 500 fast and fabulous
5-star 5-ingredient recipes.
    TX833.5.B48776 2007b
    641.5'55--dc22   2007006496

On the cover: Tangy Tequila Chicken Fettuccini, page 121,
and Toasty Dog Wedges, page 39.
Cover photos by Greg Campbell.
Illustrations by Tupper England. Design by Cynthia Clark.
Printed by Tara TPS in South Korea.

Ringbound edition (ISBN 978-1-934193-05-1)
First printing: 10,000 copies, April 2007

Paperbound edition (ISBN 978-1-893062-99-3)
First printing: 10,000 copies, January 2007
Second printing: 15,000 copies, March 2007

QUAIL RIDGE PRESS
P. O. Box 123 • Brandon, MS 39043
email: info@quailridge.com • www.quailridge.com

Contents

500

Fast and Fabulous

FIVE ★ STAR

5

INGREDIENT

Recipes

Preface

Why, with all the recipes from all over the country that Barbara Moseley and I have researched, edited, and cooked for more than three decades, did we want to write a five-ingredient cookbook?

The answer is simple: Today everybody wants *easy.*

"How can I get dinner on the table more quickly?"

"Please give us recipes that we can prepare without a lot of fuss."

"Can you make my life less complicated in the kitchen?"

Yes, we can! And your helping hand is right here! We hope to assure you that by just holding this cookbook, you will realize that you have five fingers full of fabulous recipes right at your fingertips. You can make any recipe in this book with just five ingredients! We feel that the shorter list of ingredients makes for shorter instructions, meaning you will naturally be able to keep your shopping time, prep time, and overall time in the kitchen to a minimum.

As always, our BEST OF THE BEST criteria for recipe inclusion in this cookbook is threefold: taste, taste, and *taste.*

This cookbook is comprised of recipes that we found to be not only quick to prepare, but taste-tested with come-back-for-more, let's-make-it-again goodness. Each recipe has only five ingredients, the only exceptions being salt and pepper to taste—which we figure everybody keeps on hand—and water, unless any of these is for a specific amount. For instance, if you have to boil potatoes in water to cover, we don't count water as an ingredient. But if a cake calls for 1⅓ cups of water, that water is an ingredient, and we don't want you to forget to include it.

Where did we get these recipes? They have come from friends, relatives, and customers who have graciously shared their easy-to-make recipes with us. Many have come from our personal collections. Others from favorite recipes handed down to us that we have sometimes shortened and modernized by utilizing packaged ingredients for simplicity. And our recipe testing committee, headed by Melinda Burnham, who are all so adept at trying new things, has

been excited to contribute their favorites that are—guess what?—*easy*, because that is how they also like to cook!

There are times when a recipe contributor suggests substitutions or enhancements, and we have included these in our Editor's Extras comments below their recipes. And we feel this makes it even easier, since it confirms that the recipe will be just as delicious with Swiss cheese as Cheddar, or with apples instead of peaches. Or if you happen to have whipped cream to put a dollop on a slice of pie, it may make it more special, but it is delicious without it, as well.

We decided to expand our five ingredient recipes to include a "five" theme throughout the book. We thank our research editor, Terresa Ray, for finding interesting quips and facts about the fascinating "Number 5" as an added bonus for those of you who like to read cookbooks. And thanks to our designer, Cyndi Clark, and our artist, Tupper England, who lent their talents in giving you visual "fivers" as well.

And if you're counting to see if there really are 500 recipes here, we admit there are not exactly 500—there are more! And every one was too good to pull out just for the sake of rounding the number. We figured you wouldn't mind getting a few extra.

"Could somebody please give me a helping hand?"

You bet-cha! Reach for this cookbook the next time someone hungrily asks, "What's for dinner?" Tell them simply: "Gimme five."

Gwen McKee

Fast
and
Fabulous

FIVE ★ STAR

Beverages & Appetizers

Get-Started-In-The-Mornin' Power Drink

¾ cup milk
¾ cup orange or apple juice
1 (6-ounce) container flavored yogurt
1 ripe banana, or 4 strawberries
⅓ cup soy protein powder

Blend all in blender 1 full minute. Makes 2 large glasses.

Editor's Extra: Fun to mix different flavors of yogurt with fruit. Peaches are good, too.

Cool Banana Shake

2 bananas, sliced
⅓ cup lemon juice
1 cup water
1 (14-ounce) can sweetened condensed milk
2 cups crushed ice

In blender container, combine bananas, lemon juice, water, and milk. Blend 1 minute, then add ice and blend till smooth. Makes 3–4 servings.

Blender Orange Creamsicle

Puts sunshine on your face . . . and in your body.

1 (6-ounce) can frozen orange juice concentrate
1 cup water
1 cup milk
⅓ cup sugar
1 teaspoon vanilla extract

Put all ingredients along with 10 ice cubes in blender. Blend until thick and slushy. Serves 3–4.

Lovely Lime Luscious

This is really cool!

4 cups milk, divided
¼ cup light brown sugar
1 (3-ounce) package vanilla instant pudding mix
¼ cup lime juice
4 scoops lime sherbet

In blender, food processor, or electric mixer, combine ¼ cup milk with sugar; blend in remaining milk. Add pudding mix and beat till smooth. Blend in lime juice, and pour into 4 glasses. Float a scoop of lime sherbet on top. Garnish with mint sprigs, if desired.

Creamy Sherbet Margaritas

Taste of the Caribbean.

Juice of 2 limes
⅓ cup powdered sugar
1 pint lime sherbet (4 large scoops)
4 shots good tequila
2 shots Triple Sec or Cointreau

Put all ingredients in blender, and blend with 24 ice cubes till frothy. Serve immediately. Makes 4.

Shawn's Margaritas

Party in a glass!

¾ blender full of ice cubes
1 (6-ounce) can frozen lime juice
⅔ can tequila
⅓ can Triple Sec
⅔ can water

Blend till slushed. Serve in margarita glasses; offer with or without salt around the rim. Makes 4.

The **five** basic tastes are sweet, salty, sour, bitter, and umami, which means savoury.

Everyone's tastes are different. In fact, tastes change as we get older. Babies have taste buds not only on their tongues, but on the sides and roof of their mouths. As we age, taste buds disappear from the sides and roof of our mouths, leaving taste buds mostly on your tongue.

The human tongue has about 10,000 taste buds. In general, girls have more tastebuds than boys.

The word "punch" comes from the Hindustani word for **five**. Being true to the designation of punch, the drink **Five Alive** is named for its **five** ingredients. The original citrus version included orange, lemon, grapefruit, tangerine, and lime flavors blended together.

Once widely available in the United States, **Five Alive** is now difficult to find. It is, however, still widely distributed in Canada and the United Kingdom.

Hawaiian Punch is the name of a brand of fruit punch drinks containing **5%** fruit juice. It was created in 1934 as an ice cream topping, and customers later discovered that it was an appealing drink when mixed with water.

Green Tea Punch with a Punch

This can be served as a liqueur, or over ice as a "highball."

6 lemons
4 cups sugar
3 cups strong green tea, cold
1 cup dark rum
1 cup bourbon

In large pitcher, squeeze lemon juice over sugar; add rinds. Add cold tea, and stir well. Let stand at room temperature 2 hours. Strain, then add rum and bourbon. Serve in liqueur glasses or over ice. Makes 8–10 tall glasses.

Frangelico Smoothie

Late afternoon . . . after dinner . . . home from the theatre . . . an elegant treat.

2 scoops premium vanilla ice cream
3 tablespoons half-and-half
3 tablespoons Frangelico liqueur
1 tablespoon dark crème de cocoa
Whipped cream for garnish

Mix ice cream, half-and-half, liqueur, and crème de cocoa in a blender or smoothie maker until creamy smooth. Top with whipped cream.

Editor's Extra: A sprinkle of nutmeg makes this extra special.

Easy Homemade Kahlúa

An inexpensive way to have an expensive liqueur on hand. Serve over ice cream, or in liqueur glasses with a cream floater for an exquisite finish to a meal.

2 cups water
⅓ cup instant coffee crystals
4½ cups sugar
1 tablespoon vanilla extract
1 fifth vodka

In large pot, boil water, then add coffee crystals and sugar. Simmer 15 minutes. Add vanilla, stir, and allow to cool completely. Add vodka, stir, then pour into 2 fifth bottles, preferably with dark glass. Cork well. This gets even better with age.

The Very Best Eggnog

This can be made the day before and refrigerated. Lovely in a footed glass bowl.

1 dozen large eggs, separated
2 cups sugar, divided
2 cups bourbon (or to taste)
2 quarts heavy whipping cream
1 teaspoon freshly grated nutmeg

In mixing bowl, beat egg yolks with 1½ cups sugar until mixture is lemon colored. Slowly add bourbon, beating constantly.

In second mixing bowl, beat egg whites and remaining sugar until mixture is almost stiff. Gently stir bourbon mixture into egg whites.

In large mixing bowl, whip cream, and gradually add to egg mixture. Grate fresh nutmeg over top. Serves a bunch!

Hot Chile Cups

A fun finger food everybody loves.

2 eggs
½ cup milk
1 cup shredded Cheddar or Monterey Jack cheese
1 (4-ounce) can chopped green chiles
1 (8-count) can flaky biscuits

Mix eggs well, then blend in milk, cheese, and green chiles. Separate each biscuit into 3 layers; press into miniature muffin cups. Fill with chile mixture. Bake at 375° for 20 minutes. Makes 24.

Pretty and Popular Cucumber Rounds

A new twist on an old classic.

1 package dry ranch dressing
1½ cups mayonnaise
¾ cup buttermilk
Bread rounds
2 large cucumbers, sliced

Blend first 3 ingredients. Spread on bread rounds; top with cucumber slices. May top with additional dressing and/or another bread round. If serving open face, you may want to spice them up with a sprinkle of paprika and/or red pepper. Chill.

Editor's Extra: Cucumbers are prettier unpeeled if served open-face, but you may like them peeled. How thick you slice them affects taste, too. My preference is to slice them paper thin and use several slices on each bread round—the choice is yours.

Dainty Pineapple Sandwiches for a Crowd

So easy to make—an all-time favorite.

2 (8-ounce) packages cream cheese, softened
1 cup sugar
2 (8-ounce) cans crushed pineapple, drained
1½ cups chopped pecans
2 loaves white bread, crusts removed

Blend cream cheese and sugar till fluffy. Stir in pineapple and pecans. Spread mixture on half the bread slices; top with remaining bread slices. Place sandwiches on a tray, cover with plastic wrap, and chill.

When ready to serve, cut sandwiches into fourths. Makes a bunch; can halve recipe, if desired.

Ham and Asparagus Roll-Ups

2 sheets frozen puff pastry, thawed
1 (16-ounce) package deli-sliced ham
2 cups shredded Swiss cheese
2 (8-ounce) tubs whipped chive and onion cream cheese
1 (15-ounce) can asparagus spears, drained

Preheat oven to 375°. Roll each pastry sheet into a 12x16-inch rectangle. Cut each into 16 (2x6-inch) rectangles. Down the center of 3 slices of ham, layer 1 tablespoon cheese, 1 tablespoon cream cheese, and 1 asparagus spear, making 16; roll up. Place roll-ups on pastry rectangles, then top with another pastry; seal edges. Bake on a greased baking pan about 20 minutes, or till golden brown. Makes 16.

There are **five** senses that help us interact with others and get around in our daily lives. With our **five** senses, we can see, hear, smell, touch, and taste. All of these **five** relate to food. For instance, you can see how delicious the trifle looks. You can hear the steak sizzling; you can smell the turkey roasting; you can feel how crispy the cookies are; of course with all foods, it's all about the *taste*.

Marvelous Mini Crab Cakes

1 pound fresh crabmeat, drained, flaked
½ cup dry bread crumbs
2 tablespoons mayonnaise
2 teaspoons Old Bay Seasoning
2 tablespoons chopped fresh parsley

Preheat oven to 400°. Mix crabmeat, bread crumbs, mayonnaise, seasoning, and parsley. Shape into 1½-inch patties. Bake on nonstick baking sheet 8–10 minutes. Excellent on large round wheat crackers with a dollop of tartar sauce on top.

Crab Roll-Um Bites

½ cup mayonnaise
1½ tablespoons dried onion flakes
1 cup shredded Cheddar cheese
1 (5-ounce) can white crabmeat, drained
1 (10-count) package large flour tortillas

Combine mayonnaise, onion flakes, cheese, crabmeat, and salt and pepper to taste; mix well. Spread thinly on tortillas; roll up and slice into diagonal slices. Serve now or cold. Best if made a day ahead, rolled, and wrapped. Easier to wrap unsliced rolls, then slice before serving, as they be easier to handle. Makes about 70 bites.

Parmesan Tasties

1 loaf party rye bread
1 cup freshly grated Parmesan cheese
4 green onions, chopped, some tops included
⅓ cup (or more) mayonnaise
Paprika for sprinkling

On a cookie sheet or shallow baking pan, arrange sliced bread. Mix Parmesan cheese, green onions, and mayonnaise, enough to make a spread. Spread a teaspoonful on each bread slice. Sprinkle with paprika. Broil until toasty brown.

Pizza Tizzas

Kids love this for lunch . . . or anytime. Always a hit.

Flour tortillas
Pizza sauce
Sliced pepperoni
Grated mozzarella cheese
Grated Parmesan cheese

Place desired number of tortillas on baking sheet(s). Spread each with a generous tablespoon of pizza sauce, pepperoni slices, and cheeses. Bake in 425° oven 6–8 minutes, just till bubbly and browned on edges. Cut into wedges with pizza cutter or scissors.

Editor's Extra: Good with any kind of grated cheese, salsa or spaghetti sauce, black olives, peppers, onions, or any of your favorite pizza toppings.

Bagel Pepperoni Pizzas

Nice to make on mini bagels.

½ cup pizza sauce
4 bagels, split into halves
1 cup shredded cheese blend, divided
¼ cup sliced black olives
¼ cup chopped pepperoni

Preheat oven to 425°. Spread pizza sauce evenly over each bagel half. Sprinkle each with cheese, then olives, then pepperoni. Top with more cheese. Bake on cookie sheet for 8 minutes, or until cheese melts.

Today, "pizza" is a common part of the international food vocabulary, but it is only in the last **fifty** years that both the name and the food itself have acquired widespread popularity.

Where did it originate? Around **500** BC during the Persion Empire, soldiers baked a flat bread on their shields, and covered it with cheese and dates. According to Cato the Elder, who wrote the first history of Rome around 200 BC, they ate a flat round of dough, which was baked on stones, and was dressed with olive oil, herbs, and honey. In 79 AD in the ashes that smothered Pompeii, evidence was found of shops with marble slabs that resembled pizzerias. Cooks from Naples added tomatoes from "the New World" in 1522 . . . and the rest is history.

Pimento Cheese Pizza

4 tablespoons mayonnaise
1 cup shredded Cheddar cheese
2 tablespoons finely minced onion
1 (2-ounce) jar chopped pimento
2 (7-inch) refrigerated pizza crusts

Preheat oven to 450°. Stir together mayonnaise, cheese, onion, and pimento. Cut pizza crusts into 6 wedges and place on baking sheets. Spread with cheese mixture. Bake 10 minutes or until golden brown. Serve hot.

Fruit and Nut Cheese Puffs

2 cups shredded sharp Cheddar cheese,
room temperature
½ cup butter or margarine, softened
1 cup self-rising flour
1 cup chopped dates
½ cup chopped nuts

Mix cheese and butter; stir in flour until blended. Add dates and nuts. Shape into small balls; place on ungreased baking sheet. Bake at 375° for 15–20 minutes. Makes 5 dozen.

Tiny Tasty Reubens

½ pound deli-sliced corned beef
¼ pound sliced Swiss cheese
⅔ cup Thousand Island or Catalina dressing
1 pack party rye bread
1½ cups chopped sauerkraut, well drained

Cut corned beef and cheese to size of bread. Spread dressing on bread slices. Place slices of corned beef on bread; top with sauerkraut. Place cut cheese slices on top. Bake on cookie sheet at 375° for 10 minutes, or until cheese melts.

Homemade Spiced Crackers

You have to try this one—so easy, and will keep for several days or even weeks!

1 (4-pack) box Ritz Crackers, divided
1 package dry ranch dressing mix, divided
2 tablespoons red pepper flakes (more or less to taste), divided
½ teaspoon seasoned salt
1½ cups canola oil

Place 2 packs crackers in gallon jug (you don't have to keep them stacked). Pour half a pack of ranch dressing and 1 tablespoon red pepper flakes over crackers in jug. Place other 2 packs crackers in jug, and pour remaining ranch dressing, red pepper flakes, and seasoned salt over crackers. Pour canola oil over crackers and put lid on jug. Lay jug on side and roll gently a few times; repeat every 15 minutes for a few hours. Roll jug to coat crackers and let them absorb flavors and oils. When absorbed, store crackers in zipper bag or plastic container.

The number of basketball players on the court at a given time is **five** from each team. **Five** is also the number used in basketball to represent the position of center.

5

The Pentagon is the headquarters of the United States Department of Defense. Located in Arlington, Virginia, its mailing address is "Washington, DC 20301." The building, dedicated on January 15, 1943, is the high-est-capacity office building in the world and one of the world's largest buildings in terms of floor area. It houses approximately 26,000 military and civilian employees. It has **five** sides, **five** floors above ground (plus two basement levels), and **five** ring corridors per floor with a total of 17.5 miles of corridors.

At **five** acres, the central plaza is the world's largest "no-salute, no-cover" area (exempt from the normal rule that, when out of doors, U.S. mili-tary personnel must wear hats and salute superior officers).

Classic Cheese Straws

½ pound sharp Cheddar cheese, grated
1 stick butter, softened
1½ cups all-purpose flour
½ teaspoon salt
Cayenne pepper to taste

Mix, then squeeze all ingredients together well to make a long roll. Refrigerate until hard; slice thinly. Bake on cookie sheet at 375° for 10–15 minutes, until lightly browned.

Editor's Extra: For a variation, roll dough to ⅛-inch thick-ness. Cut into strips with knife on cutting board.

Crisp Criss-Cross Cheese Wafers

A tailgate favorite. So nice to take anywhere.

½ cup butter, softened
1 cup grated sharp Cheddar cheese
1 cup all-purpose flour
1 cup Rice Krispies
⅛ teaspoon cayenne pepper, or to taste

Preheat oven to 375°. Cream butter. Stir in cheese, then flour. Stir in cereal and cayenne. Form into balls and place on cookie sheet. Flatten balls with a fork, making a criss-cross pattern. Bake for 10 minutes.

The Pentagon

Blue Cheese Ball

1 (8-ounce) package cream cheese, softened
½ cup crumbled blue cheese
¼ cup chopped pimento-stuffed green olives
¼ cup finely chopped onion
1 cup chopped nuts

Mix cream cheese, blue cheese, olives, and onion, and roll into a ball. Cover with chopped nuts. Serve with your favorite crackers.

Brie with Marmalade

1 small round Brie
¼ cup orange marmalade or raspberry preserves
3 tablespoons brown sugar
⅓ cup chopped pecans
Baguette slices, toasted

Place Brie round in a shallow baking dish. Mix marmalade and brown sugar, and spread on top of Brie. Top with chopped pecans. Bake at 350° about 15 minutes, until pecans began to toast and brown. Remove from oven and spread on baguette slices.

Pineapple Cheese Ball

2 (8-ounce) packages cream cheese, softened
¼ cup chopped bell pepper
1 (20-ounce) can crushed pineapple, drained
2 tablespoons minced onion
2 cups chopped pecans, divided

In medium bowl, blend all ingredients, except ½ cup nuts. Chill 1–2 hours. Form into a ball, and roll in remaining nuts. Serve with crackers on a decorative plate.

Editor's Extra: Sub fresh pineapple for canned, then it's fun to shape the cheese ball like a pineapple (flatten the top, score it appropriately, then put the cut-off green top of the fresh pineapple on top. Surround with crackers on a pretty plate. Pretty and delicious.

Heavenly Deviled Eggs

5 hard-boiled eggs
¼ cup mayonnaise
2 tablespoons sweet pickle relish (or dill)
¼ teaspoon salt
¼ teaspoon pepper

Peel eggs, and split in half lengthwise. Scoop yolks out into a small bowl, and mash with mayonnaise until smooth. Add pickle relish, salt, and pepper, and blend until creamy, adding more mayonnaise, if desired. Garnish with paprika.

Editor's Extra: For eggs with a little more "devil," add a little dry mustard or cayenne pepper.

Dunkin' Devil Dip

1 cup cottage cheese
1 cup sour cream
½ package onion soup mix
1 (4½-ounce) can deviled ham
1 round bread loaf

Blend cottage cheese and sour cream; add onion soup mix and deviled ham. Mix well; chill. Cut circle, square, or star from the center of bread loaf, being careful not to cut all the way through. Cut center bread chunk into cubes for dunking; toast lightly. Place deviled ham mixture in hollow center of bread. Serve with toasted bread cubes, and allow guests to cut chunks from loaf to spread with mixture.

Melinda's Crab Dip

½ (12-ounce) package frozen seasoning blend
1 (10¾-ounce) can cream of mushroom soup
2 (6-ounce) rolls garlic cheese
1 (4-ounce) jar sliced mushrooms, drained
1 pound fresh white lump crabmeat or imitation
  crabmeat

Combine all ingredients in crockpot, and allow cheese to melt. Stir until well blended, and serve warm with Ritz Crackers.

Editor's Extra: If you can't find frozen seasoning blend in the frozen vegetable section of your grocery store, you can make up your own mix of chopped onions, bell peppers, celery, and parsley.

There are four cardinal points (north, south, east, and west) according to modern Western thinking, but the Irish, along with several other traditional Indo-European cultures and the Chinese, think in terms of **five** directions—the **fifth** being "here" or "center."

5-Minute Dip

Recipes doubles easily.

1 cup sour cream
1 tablespoon prepared mustard
1 tablespoon chili sauce
½ teaspoon curry powder
¼ teaspoon Greek seasoning

Combine all ingredients. Chill and serve with pretzels, celery sticks, carrot sticks, and/or sliced cucumbers.

Creamy Dalmation Dip

1 (8-ounce) tub whipped cream cheese
1 (4-ounce) can chopped ripe olives
2 tablespoons finely chopped onion
1 teaspoon garlic salt
1 teaspoon cumin

Combine cream cheese with remaining ingredients. Good with flavored crackers or tostadas.

Five was the number of Terry Labonte's Chevy when he won the 1996 NASCAR Nextel Cup championship. Kyle Busch now has this number.

Outstanding Spinach Dip

Throw ingredients in a crockpot and let the flavors come to life.

1 (10-ounce) box frozen chopped spinach, thawed, drained well
1 (14-ounce) can marinated artichoke hearts, drained, chopped
½ cup Alfredo sauce
½ cup mayonnaise
1½ cups shredded Havarti cheese

Squeeze spinach to remove any excess moisture. Combine with remaining ingredients in a crockpot. Cover and cook on LOW 2–3 hours. Season with salt and pepper to taste.

Creamy Broccoli Dip

1 (10-ounce) package frozen broccoli florets, thawed, drained, chopped
1 (16-ounce) carton sour cream
½ cup mayonnaise
½ cup shredded sharp Cheddar cheese
1 envelope ranch dressing mix

In medium bowl, mix ingredients until thoroughly blended. Refrigerate until serving time. Serve with chips, or on bread as finger sandwiches.

Parmesan Onion Dip

3 (8-ounce) packages cream cheese, softened
3 cups grated Parmesan cheese
½ cup mayonnaise
½ teaspoon Tabasco
1½ cups chopped onions

Mix cream cheese, Parmesan, mayonnaise, and Tabasco. Stir in onions. Bake in lightly greased casserole at 425° until slightly browned, about 15 minutes. Serve hot with Fritos or Tostitos Scoops.

Chili-Cheese Hotty

1 (15-ounce) can chili (no beans)
1 (4-ounce) can chopped green chiles
1 pound Velveeta cheese, cubed
1 tablespoon Worcestershire
¼ teaspoon cumin

Combine all ingredients. Heat over low heat, stirring occasionally, until cheese melts. Serve heated with corn chips. Makes 4 cups.

Cheesy Tamale Dip

1 (1-pound) package Velveeta, cubed
1 (10-ounce) can Ro-Tel tomatoes, undrained
1 can beef tamales, wrapping removed, chopped
1 can chili with beans
1 bunch green onions, chopped

In a large nonstick saucepan or a slow cooker, melt Velveeta cubes. Add remaining ingredients and heat thoroughly. Serve with tortilla chips. Great for nachos!

Texicali Dip

1 (8-ounce) package cream cheese, softened
1 (14-ounce) can chili with beans
½ package taco seasoning mix
1 (4-ounce) can sliced black olives, drained
1 cup shredded Monterey Jack cheese

Preheat oven to 400°. In 1½-quart baking dish, layer ingredients in order given. Heat for 10–15 minutes to melt cheese. Serve with Doritos or Fritos Scoops.

Mexi-Cajun Guacamole

4 ripe avocados, peeled, halved, seeded
1–2 tablespoons lemon juice
½ cup salsa
¼ cup sour cream
1 teaspoon Cajun seasoning

Mash avocado with a fork; add lemon, salsa, sour cream, and seasoning. Mix well. Serve with tortilla chips.

Savannah's Salsa

Homemade . . . made easier!

1 (16-ounce) jar salsa
3 Roma tomatoes
¼ teaspoon Tabasco
⅓ cup finely chopped purple onion
2 tablespoons chopped fresh cilantro

Blend or process ingredients together, adding salt and pepper to taste, if desired. Serve at room temperature or chilled with tortilla chips.

Perfect Pimento Cheese Spread

1 (1-pound) block sharp Cheddar cheese, grated
1 (4-ounce) jar pimentos, diced, drained
1 (8-ounce) package cream cheese, softened
1 tablespoon Worcestershire
3 tablespoons mayonnaise (or more)

Mix cheese, pimentos, and cream cheese in mixing bowl. At low speed of mixer, slowly add Worcestershire and mayonnaise. When blended, increase speed and continue to mix until of desired spreading consistency, adding more mayonnaise, if desired.

Gingery Almond Chicken Spread

This is big-time good!

2–3 tablespoons chicken broth
⅓ cup sliced blanched almonds
¾ teaspoon powdered ginger
⅓ cup mayonnaise
1 cup cooked chopped chicken

Place broth and almonds in mini food processor or blender, and blend until smooth. Add remaining ingredients; blend again until smooth. Chill in a covered container until ready to serve. Serve with crackers or toasted bread rounds.

Editor's Extra: Nice to sub curry powder for the ginger, or use both.

Outstanding Olive Spread

12 large pimento-stuffed olives
⅓–½ cup mayonnaise
1 (8-ounce) package cream cheese, softened
2 teaspoons lemon juice
½ teaspoon hot sauce

Process ingredients in food processor till well blended. If necessary, add more mayonnaise to achieve desired consistency. Serve with your favorite crackers or vegetables.

Sea Scamp Shrimp Spread

A sure-fire winner . . . it disappears.

1 (3-ounce) package cream cheese, softened
1 cup sour cream
2 teaspoons lemon juice
1 (0.7-ounce) package Italian dressing mix
1 (4½-ounce) can shrimp, rinsed, drained

Put all ingredients in blender container, and blend until smooth. Refrigerate a few hours before serving with crackers.

A **Category 5** hurricane, with winds greater than **155** mph, is the maximum category (and the most damaging) on the Saffir-Simpson Hurricane Scale.

Category 5 hurricanes are rare with only three hitting the USA since 1928 when records began. These hurricanes were:

- Florida Keys "Labor Day" hurricane in September 1935.
- Camille hit Mississippi in August 1969.
- Andrew hit Florida on August 1992.

Multiple **Category 5** hurricanes have formed in only three seasons (1960, 1961, and **2005**), and only in **2005** have more than two formed, all failing to reach land as a **Category 5**.

Although Katrina was the costliest and one of the deadliest hurricanes in U.S. history, it weakened to a Category 4 as it approached landfall on the Mississippi/ Louisiana coast in August **2005**.

Leo is the **fifth** astrological sign of the zodiac (July 24th thru August 23rd).

Individuals born under this sign are thought to have a proud, honest, gener-ous, self-motivated, charismatic, warm-hearted, and enthusias-tic character, but one which is also prone to conceit, bullying, rigidi-ty, intolerance, and snobbery.

In mythology, Leo is often associated with the Greek myth of the Nemean Lion, who was killed by Herucles dur-ing one of his twelve labors, and subsequent-ly put into the sky as a constellation.

Spinach-Stuffed Tomatoes

So good . . . so good for you.

4 medium tomatoes, or 24 cherry tomatoes
3 handfuls fresh baby spinach
¾ cup Italian bread crumbs
½ teaspoon minced garlic
⅛ teaspoon red pepper

Cut top off tomatoes; scoop out seeds with a tea-spoon and put into a bowl. In processor, pulse spinach leaves to chop, then add bread crumbs, garlic, and red pepper. (If too stiff, add some of the tomato pulp to moisten.) Stuff tomatoes. Place on cookie sheet, and bake 15 minutes at 400°.

Editor's Extra: Like BLT's? Add a sprinkle of bacon bits and have yummy little BSTs.

The Ultimate Potato Skins

8 small russet potatoes
¾ stick butter, melted
½ pound bacon, cooked, crumbled
1 (8-ounce) package shredded sharp Cheddar cheese
½ cup sour cream

Preheat oven to 425°. Wash potatoes, and pat dry. Brush with small amount of melted butter (or oil). Bake 50–60 minutes, or till done. Remove from oven, and lower heat to 300°.

Cool potatoes slightly, then cut in half and scoop out centers. (Can reserve pulp for another dish.) Brush potato skins with melted butter. Bake in 300° oven 25 minutes. Sprinkle with bacon and cheese dur-ing last 5 minutes. Serve with sour cream.

Green Onion Bites

3 cups Bisquick
1 cup beer
¾ cup sour cream
1 envelope green onion dip mix
1 egg

Preheat oven to 400°. Stir together Bisquick and beer, mixing well. Spoon mixture into a greased 1½-quart baking dish. In small bowl, stir together sour cream, green onion dip mix, and egg. Spread over dough. Bake 20 minutes, then cut into small squares and serve warm.

A Pan Full of Loaded Nachos

1 large bag tortilla chips
1 (15-ounce) can black beans, drained
2 tablespoons chopped jalapeños,
   or 1 (4-ounce) can chopped green chiles
1 small tomato, chopped
½ pound Pepper Jack or Sonoma Jack cheese,
   shredded

Preheat broiler. Spread chips onto 2 (10x15-inch) jelly-roll pans. Sprinkle with beans, jalapeños, and tomato. Cover evenly with cheese. Broil 3–5 minutes. Remove from oven and serve immediately with a dab of sour cream on top of each loaded chip, if desired.

Game Day Appetizer

1 pound ground beef
½ cup taco sauce
½ cup mayonnaise-style salad dressing
¼ cup chopped onion
1¼ cups shredded sharp Cheddar cheese, divided

Brown meat; drain. Add combined taco sauce and salad dressing; mix well. Stir in onion and ¾ cup cheese. Spoon into a 9-inch pie plate; top with remaining cheese. Bake at 350° for 15 minutes. Serve with corn chips or crackers. Yields 4½ cups.

Tangy Frankies

½ cup red currant jelly
½ cup prepared brown mustard
2 tablespoons minced onion
1 tablespoon Worcestershire
1 pound hot dogs, cut into 1-inch chunks

Mix jelly, mustard, onion and Worcestershire in a saucepan, and bring to a boil. Add hot dogs; return to boiling. Reduce heat and simmer, covered, for 15 minutes, stirring occasionally. Keep hot in a chafing dish with cocktail picks alongside. Makes about 50 hors d'oeuvres.

Grilled Sausage Bites

12 hot-dog-size smoked sausages, cut into bite-size
 pieces
1 cup apple jelly
¼ cup ketchup
1 tablespoon yellow mustard
Hot sauce to taste

Mix sausage with remaining ingredients, and marinate in a zipper bag. Grill on skewers until heated through.

Sausage Stars

1 pound ground sausage
1 cup grated sharp Cheddar cheese
2 cups grated Monterey Jack cheese
1 cup ranch salad dressing
1 package frozen won ton wrappers

Brown sausage, and drain. Preheat oven to 350°. Cut each won ton wrapper in quarters, and fit into greased muffin tins. Stir together sausage, cheeses, and dressing. Fill won tons with sausage mixture and bake for 5–7 minutes.

Editor's Extra: Add chopped black olives for a variation.

Peppery Sausage Cheese Balls

1 roll hot bulk pork sausage, uncooked
3 cups Bisquick
1 (12-ounce) package shredded Cheddar cheese
2 teaspoons pepper
¼ teaspoon cayenne pepper

Preheat oven to 350°. Combine sausage, Bisquick, cheese, and peppers. Form into walnut-size balls. Place on a baking sheet with sides, and bake at 350° for 15–18 minutes.

Mexi Mix

4 cups Corn Chex cereal
2½ cups halved pretzel sticks
1 cup mixed nuts
1 stick butter, melted
½ package taco seasoning mix

Combine cereal, pretzels, and nuts in large bowl. In a small bowl, mix butter and seasoning mix. Pour over cereal mixture; toss to coat. Pour into ungreased extra large jellyroll pan. Bake 1 hour in 250° oven, stirring every 15 minutes. Cool completely before storing.

Many countries have **five cent coins**, but only two countries have a **five cent** coin called a **nickel**: the United States and Canada.

The Canadian **nickel**, introduced in 1922, is patterned on the corresponding coin in the United States. Prior to that year, Canadian **five-cent** pieces were small silver coins, colloquially known as "fish scales" because they were so thin.

In Ontario there is a thirty-foot replica of a 1951 Canadian **nickel** on the grounds of Dynamic Earth, an earth sciences exhibition focusing on the local mining heritage. The *Guinness Book of Records* lists it as the world's largest coin.

Canada is the third largest producer of **nickel** in the world, after Russia and Australia. The United States is Canada's largest customer for refined nickel.

Jazzy Jezebel

1 (12-ounce) jar apple jelly
1 (12-ounce) jar apricot preserves
2 tablespoons dry mustard
2 tablespoons horseradish
1 teaspoon coarse black pepper

Combine ingredients. Serve over cream cheese, or ham, or with cheese slices and crackers.

Roquefort Grapes

1 pound red seedless grapes
1 (10-ounce) package almonds, pecans, or walnuts
1 (8-ounce) package cream cheese, softened
4 tablespoons Roquefort cheese
2 tablespoons heavy cream

Wash the grapes and pat dry. Chop nuts fine. Spread on wax paper. Mix cream cheese, Roquefort cheese, and cream, and beat till smooth. Roll grapes in cheese mixture and gently press cheese mixture around each grape. Coat cheese with nuts. Place on wax paper-lined tray; chill, covered, until serving time. Leftover cheese mixture can be frozen for later use. Serves 12.

Fast
and
Fabulous

FIVE ★ STAR

Bread & Breakfast

Using the Latin root "**quin**," a **quintet** is a formation containing **five** members. It is commonly associated with musical groups, such as a string **quintet**, or a group of **five** singers, but can be applied to any situation where **five** similar or related objects are considered a single unit.

Ham and Swiss Mmmmelts

Make now . . . eat later. Or now. Delicious!

6 hamburger buns
½ stick butter, softened
1 (6-ounce) package deli-sliced ham
6 slices Swiss cheese
1 (7-ounce) can sliced mushrooms, drained

Split buns in half, and spread with butter. Divide ham, cheese, and mushrooms, and layer on bottom buns. Put on bun tops. Wrap in foil and bake at 350° for 10 minutes. If refrigerated, bake 5 minutes longer.

Editor's Extra: Muenster cheese is a good sub for the Swiss. Offer flavored mustard, pickles, and chips.

Taco-Flavored Grilled Cheese Sandwiches

A Mexican flare on an old favorite.

4 tablespoons butter, softened
2 teaspoons taco seasoning mix
4 thick slices Mexican Velveeta cheese
8 slices bread
1 cup salsa

Mix butter and taco seasoning. Place each slice cheese between 2 slices bread, making 4 sandwiches. Spread both sides of sandwiches with seasoned butter. In large skillet or griddle over medium heat, grill sandwiches 3–4 minutes on each side, or till cheese is melted and bread is golden. Cut in half and dip in salsa. Serves 4.

Crais-y Chicken Salad Stack

The contrast of flavors is uniquely delicious.

1 round loaf sourdough bread
1 (1-quart) container store-bought chicken salad
1 (6-ounce) package craisins
1 medium cucumber, peeled, chopped
3 (8-ounce) tubs whipped pineapple cream cheese

Slice bread horizontally to make 3 layers. With top and bottom layers, hollow out 2 inside cavities by pulling out some bread. Mix chicken salad and craisins together and fill bottom cavity. Put second layer on and spread with chicken salad. Fill top layer of bread with chicken salad and place on top.

In blender, mix cucumber and cream cheese. Spread on top and sides of loaf. Refrigerate. Cut into wedges to serve. Serves 8–12.

Souper Good
Chicken-In-A-Biscuit Crackers

Great to snack on and "souper" good with soup.

12 cups oyster crackers
2 tablespoons dry chicken base
1 teaspoon onion powder
2 tablespoons sour cream
1 cup vegetable oil

Mix first 3 ingredients well. Toss with sour cream and oil till crackers seem evenly coated. Spread on cookie sheet and bake at 300° for 30 minutes.

Silly Shape Sesame Crackers

Fun to make, bake, and eat.

½ cup all-purpose flour
¼ teaspoon garlic salt
2 tablespoons sesame seeds
3 tablespoons cold butter
2 tablespoons ice water

Mix flour, garlic salt, and sesame seeds. Cut in cold butter until crumbly. Sprinkle ice water on mixture and mix, then form into a ball. Break off pieces and roll dough into skinny "snakes." Form into shapes or initials. Flatten a bit on ungreased cookie sheet. Bake 15 minutes at 350°.

Easy Sausage Cornbread

Almost a meal by itself.

1 (15-ounce) can cream-style corn
2 eggs
¼ cup milk
1 (12- to 14-ounce) package corn muffin mix
¼ pound bulk pork sausage, cooked, drained

Preheat oven to 400°. Combine soup, eggs and milk. Stir in muffin mix just until blended. Fold in sausage. Pour muffin mixture into greased 9-inch square baking pan or iron skillet. Bake 20 minutes or until lightly browned and toothpick inserted in center comes out clean. Serves 8.

Truly Southern Cornbread

. . . the way it has been made for decades.

2 tablespoons hot bacon grease, divided
1¾ cups self-rising cornmeal
1½ cups buttermilk
¼ teaspoon baking soda (mix with buttermilk)
1 egg

Heat 1 tablespoon bacon grease in iron skillet. Mix remaining ingredients together well, and pour into hot grease. Bake at 450° for 20–25 minutes or until golden brown.

Moist and Delicious Cornbread Muffins

You'll have a hard time eating just one.

1 cup self-rising cornmeal
1 cup sour cream
1 (8-ounce) can cream-style corn
½ cup vegetable oil
2 eggs

Preheat oven to 400°. Combine all ingredients and mix well. Spray muffin pan with nonstick vegetable spray. Pour mixture ¾ full into each muffin cup. Bake 20 minutes. Serve hot.

Did you know the animal pictured on the **Buffalo Nickel** is actually a bison, not a buffalo? Though they belong to the same family, true buffalo are native only to Africa and Asia. Because early U.S. explorers likened bison to buffalos, the name has become entrenched as a colloquialism in North American culture and language.

The U.S. "Buffalo" **Nickel** (also known as the Indian Head **Nickel**) was produced between 1913 and 1938, and was designed by James Earle Fraser.

Buffalo Nickel (1913–1938)

On almost all devices with a numeric keypad such as telephones, computers, etc., the "**5**" key has a raised dot or raised bar to make it easier for people who are blind or have low vision to be able to feel the keys. All other numbers can be found in their relative position around the "**5**" button.

Easy Egg Custard Rolls

2 packages dry yeast
1¼ cups lukewarm water
½ cup butter, melted
1 (3-ounce) package egg custard mix
3½ cups all-purpose flour

Mix ingredients in order. Knead a few turns, then shape into rolls, and let rise on greased baking sheet about 2 hours. (Or place in greased bowl in refrigerator to make later.) Bake at 400° for 12–15 minutes. Makes 24 rolls.

A Dozen Pretty Popovers

This one get a heads up!

6 eggs
¼ cup vegetable oil
2 cups milk
1¾ cups unsifted all-purpose flour
1½ teaspoons salt

Combine eggs and oil in large bowl; beat slightly. Gradually beat in milk, flour, and salt. Pour batter into 12 well-greased custard cups in a baking pan. Bake in 375° oven 50 minutes, or until golden brown.

A numeric keypad

Pull-A-Part Parmesan Wedges

These are good!

1 (8-count) can flaky jumbo biscuits
¼ cup butter, melted
2 tablespoons parsley flakes
½ tablespoon onion flakes
1 tablespoon grated Parmesan cheese

Cut biscuits into 4 wedges. Place melted butter, parsley, and onion flakes in bottom of 9-inch pie pan. Wedge biscuits in pan and sprinkle with Parmesan cheese. Bake at 425° for 20 minutes.

Toasty Dog Wedges

A delicious quick bread made with leftover hot dog buns.

½ stick butter, melted
1 teaspoon parsley flakes
½ teaspoon garlic salt
½ teaspoon cracked black pepper
4 hot dog buns, quartered lengthwise

Mix butter with seasonings and spread or brush on bread fingers. Bake in 400° oven 10–15 minutes till lightly browned.

Cheddar Pecan Biscuits

2 cups self-rising flour
1½ sticks butter, melted
1 (8-ounce) container sour cream
1 cup shredded sharp Cheddar cheese
1 cup chopped pecans

Combine flour, butter, sour cream, cheese, and pecans; blend well. Drop by heaping tablespoonfuls onto greased baking pan. Bake at 425° about 20 minutes or until golden brown.

Garlic Cheddar Cheese Drop Biscuits

2 cups biscuit mix
⅔ cup milk
½ cup shredded Cheddar cheese
½ stick butter, melted
¼ teaspoon garlic powder

In large bowl, stir together biscuit mix, milk, and cheese until soft dough forms. Beat 30 more seconds. Drop dough by rounded spoonfuls onto ungreased baking sheet. Bake at 450° about 10 minutes or till golden. Combine butter with garlic powder, and brush over hot biscuits.

BPB's (Baking Powder Biscuits)

Bring on the butter, jelly, and syrup.

2 cups sifted all-purpose flour
3 teaspoons baking powder
1 teaspoon salt
⅓ cup shortening
¾ cup milk

Preheat oven to 425°. Combine flour, baking powder, and salt. Cut in shortening until mixture resembles coarse meal. Add milk; stir with fork until blended. On a lightly floured surface, knead gently 8–10 times. Roll dough ½ inch thick. Cut with floured cutter. Bake 12–15 minutes on ungreased baking pan.

Garlic Bread . . . with Peanut Butter?

Oh yeah! Great snacker.

¼ cup smooth or crunchy peanut butter
1 garlic clove, crushed
½ cup butter or margarine, softened
Dash of salt
1 loaf French bread

Mix peanut butter with garlic, butter, and salt. Slice French bread in 1-inch slices, not quite through bottom of loaf. Spread peanut butter mixture between slices. Wrap in aluminum foil and bake in hot oven 400° for 10–15 minutes. Serve hot.

Chocolate Banana Sandwich Supreme

1 (3.5-ounce) milk chocolate candy bar
8 slices cinnamon bread
2 bananas, sliced
4 tablespoons butter, divided
⅓ cup powdered sugar

Divide candy bar into 16 pieces, placing equally over 4 slices of bread. Top each with ½ banana. Top with remaining bread. Heat 1 tablespoon butter in skillet. Carefully add sandwich, chocolate side down. Cover skillet, and cook over medium heat till golden brown on each side. Repeat with remaining sandwiches. Dust with powdered sugar.

Jim "Moose" Brown, born in Dearborn, Michigan, started playing piano by ear at age three. At twelve, Jim picked up the guitar. As an adult, Jim moved to Nashville and landed jobs playing on the road for Jim Ed Brown, Marie Osmond, Bill Anderson, and Dan Seals. Jim's career choices eventually led him to songwriting, which led to Jim's first publishing deal with SeaGayle Music in 2000. Jim's songwriting credits include the #1 smash "It's **Five** O'Clock Somewhere," performed by Alan Jackson and Jimmy Buffett.

"It's **Five** O'Clock Somewhere" tied a record with Lonestar's "Amazed" for the longest #1 song in history (eight weeks at #1), and earned Jim a Grammy Award in 2004 for Best Country Song.

Amendment V (the **Fifth Amendment**) of the United States Constitution, which is part of the Bill of Rights, is related to legal procedure. The Bill of Rights limits the powers of the federal government, protecting the rights of the people.

To "plead the **Fifth**" or to "take the **Fifth**" is to refuse to answer a question because the response could form incriminating evidence.

Oven-Baked Blender Pancakes

A really tasty square meal.

1 cup flour
6 eggs
1 cup milk
4 tablespoons butter, melted
½ teaspoon salt

Blend all ingredients in blender until well mixed. Pour into greased 9x13-inch pan. Bake at 450° for 20 minutes. Cut into squares, and serve hot.

Editor's Extra: Serve with melted butter and powdered sugar. A squeeze of fresh lemon juice is great, or opt for syrup.

Easy French Toast

5 slices Texas toast
2 eggs, beaten
⅓ cup milk
2 teaspoons cinnamon sugar
3 tablespoons butter

Cut toast in half. Mix eggs, milk, and sugar. Melt butter in skillet. Dip a piece of toast in egg/milk mixture, and fry in butter. Stir batter after each piece of toast is dipped. Cook until golden brown; serve hot with syrup.

Crockpot Apple Butter

8 cups cored, chopped, unpeeled cooking apples
1 cup apple cider
1 cup sugar
1 teaspoon ground cinnamon
1/8 teaspoon ground cloves

Cook apples and apple cider in crockpot on LOW about 10 hours. Purée in food processor or blender. Return mixture to crockpot, and add sugar, cinnamon, and cloves. Cook on LOW 1 hour. Makes 1 quart. Refrigerate unused portion in glass jar.

Dark and Lovely Blueberry Jam

Makes a lovely gift.

2 1/2 cups blueberries
3 cups sugar
1/3 cup orange juice
1 tablespoon lemon juice
1/2 (3-ounce) bottle fruit pectin

Wash blueberries and drain. Crush blueberries in an enamel or stainless steel saucepan. Mix sugar, orange juice, and lemon juice; add to pan. Boil hard for one minute, stirring constantly. Remove from heat, and stir in pectin. Seal in hot sterilized jelly jars. Refrigerate.

Cream Cheese Danish

Treat your overnight guests to a fantastic breakfast treat.

2 (8-ounce) cans crescent rolls
1½ (8-ounce) packages cream cheese, softened
1 cup sugar, divided
1 teaspoon vanilla
1 egg, separated

Press 1 can of unrolled crescent rolls in a 9x13-inch pan. Beat cream cheese until fluffy; add ¾ cup sugar, vanilla, and egg yolk; beat until creamy. Spread over crescent rolls. Press out second can of crescent rolls and place over cream cheese mixture. Brush with frothed egg white (you don't need to use all of it), and sprinkle with remaining ¼ cup sugar. Bake in 375° oven 18–20 minutes. Serves 8.

Marshmallow Breakfast Rolls

½ teaspoon cinnamon
2 tablespoons sugar
5 large marshmallows, halved
1 tablespoon butter, melted
1 (10-count) can refrigerated biscuits

Preheat oven to 375°. Combine cinnamon and sugar. Roll marshmallows in melted butter, then in sugar mixture. Wrap each marshmallow with flattened biscuit, and seal edges. (Be careful not to get sugar on edges of biscuit; it won't seal.) Bake in preheated oven 11–13 minutes or until lightly browned.

Chocolate Chip Cinnamon Breakfast Ring

A chocolate lover's idea of a super breakfast.

½ cup butter, divided
2 (12-ounce) cans cinnamon rolls with icing, divided
1 (3-ounce) box cook 'n serve vanilla pudding, divided
½ cup packed brown sugar, divided
¼ cup semisweet chocolate chips

Heat oven to 375°. Using 1 tablespoon butter, generously butter a 12-cup Bundt pan. In small microwaveable bowl, melt remaining butter on HIGH 1 minute.

Separate dough into 16 rolls. Cut each roll in half crosswise and place half in pan. Sprinkle with half pudding mix and half brown sugar. Drizzle with half the melted butter. Repeat with remaining roll pieces, pudding mix, brown sugar, and melted butter. Sprinkle with chocolate chips.

Bake 24–28 minutes or until rolls are deep golden brown, and dough appears done when slightly pulled apart. Cool in pan 2 minutes. Place heat-proof serving platter upside down over pan; turn platter and pan over. Remove pan; cool 15 minutes.

Microwave icing on HIGH 10 seconds to soften. Drizzle icing over ring. Cut into wedges; serve warm.

Five babies born at one time are **quintuplets**. The most famous set of **quintuplets** were the **Dionne Quintuplets**, who were born May 28, 1934, near Corbeil, Ontario, Canada. They were the first **quintuplets** known to have survived infancy: Annette (1934–), Cecile (1934–), Emilie (1934–1954), Marie (1934–1970), and Yvonne (1934–2001).

In the movie *Raising Arizona*, a 1987 Coen Brothers comedy film starring Nicolas Cage and Holly Hunter, the plot is largely driven by the protagonists' kidnapping of Nathan Arizona, Jr., one of a set of **quintuplets**.

Monkey Bread Breakfast

You'll wake up proud of yourself for having these rolls ready to pop in the oven.

1 (16-ounce) package frozen rolls
³/₄ stick butter, melted, divided
1 (3-ounce) package cook 'n serve butterscotch or vanilla pudding mix
¹/₂ cup packed brown sugar
1¹/₂ cups finely chopped pecans

Dip frozen rolls in melted butter; reserve remaining butter; place rolls in Bundt or tube pan. Sprinkle pudding mix, brown sugar, and pecans over rolls. Pour remaining melted butter over all. Leave on counter top overnight. Next morning, bake at 350° for 40 minutes. Invert onto platter, and start picking off the delicious warm rolls.

Dotted Swiss Muffins

Ham and cheese in a muffin!

2 cups baking mix
²/₃ cup milk
1 (5-ounce) can ground ham
1 cup shredded Swiss cheese
1 heaping tablespoon poppy seeds

Mix all ingredients and bake in large muffin tins at 400° for 10–12 minutes. Makes 9 large or 12 medium muffins.

Editor's Extra: Nice to serve with whipped pineapple cream cheese.

Spruced-Up Blueberry Muffins

Add some good-for-you ingredients to muffins at breakfast time . . . an easy and extra delicious sprucing-up of muffin mix. Good for take-along breakfasts.

1 (7-ounce) package blueberry muffin mix
²/₃ cup milk
½ ripe banana, mashed
¼ cup chopped nuts
¼ cup quick-cooking or instant oatmeal

Mix all together. Pour into 9 greased muffin cups; bake in preheated 425° oven 14–17 minutes. Butter 'em while they're hot!

Editor's Extra: Great to use strawberry or chocolate chip muffins, too.

Blueberry Muffins

2 cups biscuit mix
1 cup brown sugar
1 cup sour cream
1 egg
1 cup blueberries

Preheat oven to 350°. Combine biscuit mix, brown sugar, sour cream, egg, and blueberries in a large bowl. Fill large muffin cups ²/₃ full, and bake 20–25 minutes, or until muffins test done.

Toasty Apple Cinnamon Bread

A quick breakfast treat.

6 pieces toast, halved
½ stick butter, softened
½ cup sugar
2 teaspoons cinnamon
2 apples, peeled, cored, thinly sliced

Preheat oven to 400°. Arrange toast in a single layer in baking pan. Cream butter, sugar, and cinnamon, and spread on one side of toast. Cover toast completely with apple slices. Spread remaining butter mixture over apples. Bake 10 minutes. Put under broiler for a couple of minutes, just until sugar begins to brown. Serve hot. Serves 4–6.

Apple Cinnamon Roll Coffee Cake

Easy and impressive.

1½ cups chopped peeled apples, divided
1 (8-count) can refrigerated cinnamon rolls
⅓ cup brown sugar
2 tablespoons butter, melted
2 tablespoons corn syrup

Grease a deep-dish pie plate, and spread 1 cup apples in bottom. Separate dough into 8 rolls, and cut each roll into 4 pieces; place in large bowl with remaining ½ cup apples.

Preheat oven to 350°. In small bowl, combine brown sugar, butter, and corn syrup, and mix well. Add this mixture to roll pieces in bowl, and toss gently to coat. Spoon over apples in pan. Bake at 350° for 30 minutes or until deep golden brown. Microwave icing container (from roll package), uncovered, on HIGH for 15 seconds or until smooth. Drizzle over cake. Serves 6.

Apple Sausage Wagon Wheel Pie

Cheese, apples, sausage . . . what could be better?

1 (11-ounce) box Betty Crocker Pie Crust Mix
1 (1-pound) package small pork sausage links
1 (20-ounce) can apple pie filling
1 cup shredded Cheddar cheese
½ cup brown sugar, firmly packed

Preheat oven to 375°. Using ½ package pie crust mix, make a single pie crust. Fit into a 9-inch pie pan; flute edge and prick bottom and sides with a fork. Bake 10 minutes.

Brown sausage links; drain on paper towels.

Spoon pie filling into partially baked pie crust. Place cooked sausage, spoke-fashion, on pie filling. Sprinkle with cheese. Combine remaining ½ pie crust mix with brown sugar, and sprinkle over pie. Return to oven and bake about 30 minutes, until crust is golden brown. Serves 6.

Soft Creamy Scrambles

½ stick butter
8 eggs
¼ cup sour cream
¾ teaspoon salt
¼ teaspoon cracked black pepper

Put butter in top of double boiler over boiling water. Blend eggs, sour cream, salt, and pepper well. Pour into melted butter. Stir, scrape, and cut up the eggs while cooking until no liquid remains. Serve immediately. Serves 6.

"**Fifth wheel**" has several meanings:

- A wheel or portion of a wheel placed horizontally over the forward axle of a carriage to provide support and stability during turns

- A steering bearing that enables the front axle of a horse-drawn wagon to rotate

- A device over the rear axle or axles of a tractor or pickup truck, serving as a coupling and support for a semitrailer

- An extra and unnecessary person or thing. The **5th Wheel** is an American reality dating show based on this concept.

There are more than a hundred species of wild roses. The shrub is famous for its prickly stems with their beautiful flowers and nutritious "rosehips."

The flowers of most species have **five** petals and **five** sepals and are usually white or pink, though in a few species yellow or red.

The fruit of the rose is called a rosehip. Rose species that produce open-faced flowers like the wild rose are attractive to pollinating bees and other insects, thus more apt to produce hips. Rosehips, which have an applelike flavor, are very high in vitamin C, and are an even better source than orange juice. The rosehips can be made into teas, jams, syrups, and jellies.

All Together Light Bacon and Eggs

8 eggs, separated
1 cup half-and-half
½ teaspoon salt
¼ teaspoon celery salt or Mrs. Dash Table Blend
6 strips bacon, cooked crisp, crumbled

Preheat oven to 350°. Beat egg yolks until thick and lemon-colored. Blend in cream, seasonings, and bacon. Beat egg whites till stiff; fold into egg mixture. Pour into 8 greased custard dishes. Place in a pan of hot water, and bake uncovered 25–30 minutes or until puffy. Serves 8.

Bacon and Tomato Omelet

2 teaspoons butter
1½ slices bacon, cooked, crumbled
3 eggs, beaten
¼ cup shredded Swiss cheese
2 tablespoons diced tomato

Melt butter in nonstick skillet. Sprinkle in the bacon. Pour in the eggs. Tilt and pull back edges to allow uncooked eggs to go to the bottom of the skillet. Cook until nearly set, then sprinkle with cheese and tomato. Fold in half and remove from pan.

Breakfast Burritos Olé!

1 dozen eggs
¾ cup salsa
10 (8-inch) flour tortillas
1 cup shredded Cheddar cheese
1 (4-ounce) can green chiles

Beat eggs, then stir in salsa. Scramble eggs and salsa mixture until eggs are just set. Heat tortillas in microwave just long enough to soften. Place an even amount of egg mixture down center of each tortilla. Roll up and place in large nonstick skillet. Sprinkle with cheese and green chiles. Cover with lid and heat over medium heat until cheese melts.

Green Chile Baked Breakfast Casserole

1 pound bulk pork sausage
¾ cup grated cheese
12 eggs, beaten
¾ cup milk
2 (4-ounce) cans green chiles, chopped, drained

Brown and crumble sausage; drain. Combine sausage, cheese, eggs, milk, and chiles, then pour into a greased 2-quart casserole pan. Bake at 350° about 35 minutes.

Southern Breakfast Casserole

Bring on the biscuits!

1 cup quick grits
1 pound bulk pork sausage
½ cup chopped onion
2 eggs, beaten
1 (8-ounce) package shredded Cheddar cheese,
   divided

Cook grits according to package directions. Sauté sausage and onion in a large skillet until onion is tender, stirring to break up sausage; drain grease. Combine grits, sausage and onion, eggs, and 1½ cups cheese. Pour into a greased 9x13-inch pan. Bake 35–40 minutes. Sprinkle with remaining cheese during last 10 minutes of cook time. Serves 8.

Late-Night Breakfast Supper

2 whole English muffins
1–2 teaspoons butter for spreading
1 (16-ounce) can corned beef hash with potatoes
4 eggs
½ teaspoon salt

Split English muffins, spread lightly with butter, and toast in oven. Remove from oven and place in a greased 8x8-inch pan. Spread corned beef hash over top of muffins. Break eggs on top of corned beef hash, centering them on top of each muffin half. Bake in a 350° oven until eggs are set. Remove from oven and season to taste.

Tennessee Sawmill Gravy

A southerner comes running for this classic dish.

1 pound bulk sausage
2 tablespoons flour (or more)
1½ cups milk (or more)
½ teaspoon salt, or to taste
¼ teaspoon white pepper

Form sausage into patties; fry in moderately hot skillet until brown; drain on paper towels. Reserve ½ the grease in skillet to make gravy. Brown flour in grease, stirring constantly. Add milk gradually to achieve desired consistency. Crumble 4 cooked sausage patties into gravy. Add salt and pepper. Serve over hot biscuits with remaining sausage patties.

Ham and Red Eye Gravy

Goes great with biscuits and grits!

2 teaspoons oil or bacon drippings
8 (½-inch-thick) small ham slices
1 cup black coffee
½ teaspoon sugar
1 cup water

Heat oil or drippings in large heavy skillet till hot; add ham, and cook (in batches, if necessary) on both sides till browned. Set aside, and keep warm. Stir coffee and sugar into pan drippings, scraping bottom well; bring to a boil, then lower heat to a simmer. Simmer uncovered about 2 minutes. Serve gravy over ham.

In **2005**, as a University of Southern California football player, Reginald Alfred "Reggie" Bush II (born March 2, **1985**) was awarded the Walter Camp Award and the Doak Walker Award. A few days later, Bush also won the most prestigious award in college football, the Heisman Trophy while wearing the number **five.**

Bush elected to forgo his senior season at USC and declared himself eligible for the NFL draft. It was predicted that he would be the first overall pick in the 2006 NFL Draft. However, in a surprising move, the Houston Texans signed Mario Williams. The New Orleans Saints selected Bush with their #2 pick in the draft.

Bush now wears the number **25** as a member of the Saints, and is already making history—becoming the first rookie in NFL history to score a game-winning touchdown on a punt return in the final **five** minutes of the fourth quarter, or in overtime.

Tomato Gravy

Serve with bacon, eggs, and biscuits for a southern meal so delicious it'll make you come back beggin' for more.

1 tablespoon oil
¼ cup chopped onion
2 tablespoons all-purpose flour
1 cup stewed tomatoes
1 cup chicken broth or water

Heat oil over medium-heat in heavy skillet; sauté onion. Add flour, and stir constantly till medium brown. Add tomatoes and chicken broth or water, and stir quickly. Allow to boil for about a minute, then lower heat and simmer till thickened to desired consistency. Add salt and pepper to taste, if desired.

Fast
and
Fabulous

FIVE ★ STAR

Soups, Chilies, & Stews

The first **$5** United States Note was issued in 1862 featuring a small portrait of Alexander Hamilton. The bill has undergone many design changes throughout the years, currently featuring Abraham Lincoln's portrait with the Lincoln Memorial on the reverse side.

In 2000, to combat evolving counterfeiting, a new **$5** bill was issued under series 1999, whose design was similar in style to the $100, $50, $20, and $10 bills that had all undergone previous design changes. The **$5** bill, however, does not feature color-shifting ink like all the other denominations.

Another redesign is underway, with release expected in the first quarter of 2008.

The Bureau of Engraving and Printing says the average time a **$5** bill stays in circulation is two years before it is replaced due to wear.

Mac 'n Cheese Soup

3 cups water
2 cups milk
1 (14-ounce) package macaroni and cheese dinner
1½ cups frozen seasoning blend
½ pound Velveeta, cut up

Bring water and milk to a boil in large saucepan. Stir in macaroni (reserve cheese sauce) and vegetables. Return to a boil, then simmer 10–12 minutes or until macaroni is soft.

Add Velveeta and pouch of cheese sauce; stir until well blended. Serves 8.

Editor's Extra: If you can't find frozen seasoning blend, you can make up your own mix of chopped onions, bell peppers, celery, and parsley.

Cream of Tomato Soup Quickie

1 medium onion, chopped
2 tablespoons butter
2 tablespoons flour
1 quart tomato juice
2 cups milk, heated

In a Dutch oven over medium heat, sauté onion in butter until translucent. Remove from heat and stir in flour, then slowly whisk in tomato juice. Return to heat; add salt and pepper to taste. Turn off heat before it boils. Slowly stir in hot milk. Serve immediately. Serves 4–6.

Reproduction of Series 2003 United States five dollar bill

Leeky Creamy Potato Soup

6 medium potatoes, peeled, cubed small
1 (14-ounce) can chicken broth
1 cup chopped leeks
1 tablespoon butter
1½ cups heavy whipping cream

Boil potatoes and broth in a large pot; lower to medium heat and allow to simmer 20–25 minutes, or until potatoes are tender.

In a separate skillet over medium heat, sauté leeks in butter 5–10 minutes, or until tender. Add leeks and cream to potatoes, stir well, and heat slightly. Do not allow to boil. You may take a potato masher and mash part of the potatoes to slightly thicken the soup, if desired.

Editor's Extra: Onion or green onion can sub for the leeks. Add a sprinkle of parsley to top of each bowl when serving to give it a touch of color.

Baked Potato Soup

A classic. Nice, nice, nice.

⅓ cup butter
⅓ cup all-purpose flour
4 cups milk
6 large baking potatoes, scrubbed, baked
1 cup sour cream

Mix butter and flour in skillet on medium-high heat. Stir constantly. When roux is thickened a bit, gradually blend in milk. Continue cooking over low to medium heat (do not let boil) while preparing potatoes.

Peel and cut up potatoes; add to milk mixture. Blend in sour cream, and salt and pepper to taste. Serve immediately. Serves 8.

Editor's Extra: I like to mash some of the potatoes, too, at the cut-up stage. If you overly bake them, they're going to be pretty much mashed anyway.

Swiss Onion Soup in a Flash

1 (10¾-ounce) can cream of onion soup
1¼ cups water
¾ cup milk
2 tablespoons grated onion
⅔ cup shredded Swiss cheese

Combine soup, water, milk, and onion in a saucepan over medium heat. Stir in cheese, and bring just to a boil. Remove from heat and serve. Serves 4–6.

Verdi Tortellini

1 (10-ounce) package frozen chopped spinach,
**   thawed, drained**
2 (14-ounce) cans chicken broth
1 (9-ounce) package cheese or chicken tortellini
1 teaspoon dried basil
1½ teaspoons garlic powder

Combine spinach and chicken broth in a large pot over high heat. Heat to boiling, then reduce heat to low. Stir in tortellini, and simmer 10–15 minutes, or until tortellini is tender and has absorbed much of the broth. Season with basil and garlic powder. Add salt and pepper to taste, if desired. Serves 8.

Butter Bean and Ham Soup

A hearty, warming, wonderful soup. Good use of leftover ham.

½ pound ham, ground or minced
1 medium onion, diced small
1 carrot, peeled, diced small
2 (16-ounce) cans butter beans, undrained
4 cups water

Sauté ham and onion a few minutes in stockpot. Add carrot, butter beans, and water. Bring to a boil, then reduce heat and simmer 30–60 minutes, or more. Serves 4–6.

5

Hearty Lentil Soup

4 cups chicken broth or stock
½ cup sliced carrots
3 cloves garlic, minced
1 cup chopped onion
1 cup lentils

Add chicken broth, carrots, garlic, onion, and lentils to a 3- to 4-quart crockpot. Cook on LOW 8–10 hours, or until tender. Serves 4–6.

Black-Eyed Pea Soup

2 cups dried black-eyed peas
1 pound smoked turkey sausage, sliced
4 carrots, chopped
1 cup water
3 (14-ounce) cans beef broth

Sort, rinse, and drain peas. In large stockpot, cover peas with cold water and bring to a boil. Turn off heat, cover, and let sit for an hour. Drain peas, then rinse.

Combine with remaining ingredients in crockpot. Cook on LOW about 8 hours, until peas are tender. Season with salt and pepper to taste. Serves 6.

In **2005**, St. Louis Cardinals first baseman Albert Pujols won the National League Most Valuable Player award wearing the number **five**. Pujols (pronounced "Poo-holes") was born January 16, 1980, in the Dominican Republic. He is widely regarded as one of the best offensive players in the game. On July 13, 2006, Pujols became the first player in Major League history to hit thirty or more home runs in each of his first six seasons. On August 22nd of that year, he became the first Major League player since Ted Williams to reach the 100 RBI mark in each of his first six seasons. He is the youngest player in MLB history to hit **250** career home runs.

Five is also the retired number of former baseball players Joe DiMaggio, Hank Greenberg, Brooks Robinson, Johnny Bench, and George Brett.

The hours of a standard work day are 9 am to **5** pm. Some songs that make reference to it are "**9 to 5**," a theme song for the 1980 film comedy **Nine to Five** starring Jane Fonda, Lily Tomlin and, in her film debut, Dolly Parton. The title song, written and performed by Parton, won a Grammy Award. The song was also the centerpiece of Parton's **9 to 5 and Odd Jobs** album. The song reached #1 on both the Billboard Country Chart and Hot 100. The song became an anthem for office workers in the United States.

It is not to be confused with Sheena Easton's song "**Morning Train (Nine to Five)**," which was released a few months later.

"**Five O'clock World**" performed by The Vogues was released in 1965 and peaked at #4. It was remade by Bowling for Soup and used as the opening of *The Drew Carey Show* for a few seasons.

Cheesy Broccoli Soup

Bring on the crackers . . . or toast . . . or tostadas. Just bring it on!

1 (10-ounce) package frozen broccoli florets
3 cups chicken broth
3 cups milk, divided
2 tablespoons flour
1 (1-pound) box Velveeta, cubed

Cook broccoli in broth till tender; do not drain. In a cup, stir a small amount of milk into flour to make a loose paste, then add to broccoli with remaining milk. Stir in cheese and continue cooking over medium heat till cheese melts, stirring frequently. Serves 6.

Baby Spinach Soup

Eating your greens has never been tastier.

2 (14-ounce) cans chicken broth
¾ cup chopped onion
1½ teaspoons minced garlic
3 (9-ounce) packages baby spinach
½ cup whipping cream

Heat chicken broth in stockpot; add onion and garlic; simmer 5 minutes. Add spinach; stir to combine. Purée soup in batches in blender until smooth. Return to stockpot. Stir in whipping cream. Cook over medium heat, bringing just to a boil. Remove from heat, and season to taste with salt and pepper. Serves 4–6.

Autumn Soup

4 (14-ounce) cans chicken broth
2 (11-ounce) cans shoe peg corn, drained
1 onion, chopped
1 (16-ounce) can solid-pack pumpkin
1 cup half-and-half

In a stockpot, combine chicken broth, corn, and onion. Bring to a boil, then reduce heat to a simmer. Simmer covered about 25 minutes, until onion is tender. Whisk in pumpkin, and mix well. Cover and simmer 8 more minutes, then add half-and-half. Heat through, but do not boil. Season with salt and pepper to taste.

Sunny Squash Soup

This soup is sunny yellow and so creamy.

8 crookneck squash, chopped
1 green bell pepper, chopped
1 onion, chopped
2 cups cubed Velveeta cheese
1 teaspoon seasoning salt

Cook squash, bell pepper, and onion in a stockpot with water to cover. Bring vegetables to a boil, then reduce heat; simmer about 15 minutes, or till tender. Drain. Purée soup in blender, then return to pot. Add cheese, and heat over medium heat till cheese is melted. Season with your favorite seasoning salt blend.

Editor's Extra: Add a dash of paprika or some chopped parsley if the sun is too bright! And you don't have to purée this soup if you like your veggies visible.

Cool as a Cucumber Soup

1 medium cucumber, peeled, seeded, shredded
1 tablespoon grated onion
1 (10¾-ounce) can cream of celery soup
1 cup buttermilk
1 cup cottage cheese

In a bowl, combine cucumber and onion; strain out liquid. In a blender, blend soup, buttermilk, and cucumber and onion mixture. Add cottage cheese and blend again; season with salt and pepper to taste. Refrigerate until ready to serve. Serves 6.

Cool Red Pepper Soup

The perfect soup for a summer evening.

2 (12-ounce) jars roasted red peppers, packed in brine
1 tablespoon olive oil
1 tablespoon sugar
2 cups chicken broth
¾ cup sour cream

Drain red peppers, and cut into strips. Process pepper strips, olive oil, and sugar in food processor 20–30 seconds. With motor still running, pour chicken broth into mixture. Process until smooth. Add sour cream and process until smooth, 15–20 seconds. Refrigerate soup at least 1 hour or overnight. Garnish with minced fresh chives, if desired. Serves 6–8.

62

5

Enchilada Soup

1 (9-ounce) package frozen cooked southwestern-
flavored chicken strips, thawed
2 (10¾-ounce) cans cream of chicken soup
1 (10-ounce) can enchilada sauce
2 cups milk
1 cup shredded Cheddar cheese

Chop chicken strips. In large saucepan, combine chicken strips with soup, enchilada sauce, milk, and cheese. Cook over medium heat till heated and cheese is melted. May be topped with crushed tortilla chips, if desired.

Ten-Minute Santa Fe Soup

1 cup milk
1 (16-ounce) box Velveeta cheese, cubed
1 (15-ounce) can corn, drained
1 (15-ounce) can black beans, rinsed, drained
1 (14½-ounce) can diced tomatoes with green chiles,
undrained

Combine all in large saucepan. Stir over medium heat until cheese is melted and soup is hot, 7–10 minutes. Serves 4–6.

Editor's Extra: For even more spiciness, you can sub Mexican Velveeta, or half Mexican and half regular.

High five is a celebratory gesture made by two people, each raising one hand to slap the raised hand of the other—usually meant to communicate to spectators mutual self-satisfaction, or to extend congratulations from one person to another. The arms are usually extended into the air to form the "high" part, and the **five** fingers of each hand meet, making the "**five**."

National High Five Day falls on the third Thursday of April each year. The holiday originated at the University of Virginia in 2002, and has since spread across the nation.

A **five** o'clock shadow is beard growth visible late in the day on a man whose face was clean-shaven in the morning. The term comes from the traditional 9 am to **5** pm. workday hours.

The most famous politician in history to sport a **five** o'clock shadow, at a time when it was still considered a faux pas, was Richard Nixon, who is said to have lost the 1960 presidential election in part due to his unfortunate stubbled appearance during the televised United States presidential election debates with John F. Kennedy.

During the 1980s, the **five** o'clock shadow gained social acceptance, and grew in popularity. The style was inspired largely by the popular television series *Miami Vice*, with its lead character, James "Sonny" Crockett (Don Johnson), having an unshaven appearance at all times.

Can-tastic Salsa Soup

Too easy to be true.

3 (5-ounce) cans chicken
2 (14-ounce) cans chicken broth
2 (16-ounce) cans hominy
1 (16-ounce) jar salsa
1–2 teaspoons cumin

Empty cans into large stockpot; add salsa and cumin. Bring to a boil, then reduce heat and simmer till heated thoroughly. Serve with tostadas crumbled on top, if desired. Serves 6–8.

Easy Chicken Tortilla Soup

8 cups water
1 (9-ounce) package tortilla soup mix
4–6 chicken tenders, cut in thin strips
1 teaspoon Emeril's Essence Seasoning
1 bag tortilla chips

Bring water to a boil; stir in soup mix. Simmer soup 12–15 minutes. While soup is simmering, sprinkle chicken strips with seasoning, and lightly cook in a little oil. Add chicken strips to soup during last 5 minutes of cooking. Serve soup in bowls with broken tortilla chips.

Editor's Extra: Top with shredded Co-Jack cheese, if desired.

Anchors Away Soup

1 (14-ounce) can chicken broth
3 (15-ounce) cans navy beans, undrained
1 cup chopped ham
1 cup chopped onion
½ teaspoon seasoned salt

In a large saucepan, combine all ingredients. Bring to a boil; reduce heat and simmer until onion becomes tender. Serves 6–8.

Vegetable Beef-V Soup

1 pound lean ground beef
1 (12-ounce) package frozen seasoning blend
1 (46-ounce) bottle V-8 juice
2 (16-ounce) packages frozen mixed vegetables
¾ teaspoon black pepper

Brown and crumble ground beef with seasoning blend in a Dutch oven over medium-high heat; drain. Add juice, mixed vegetables, and black pepper. Bring to a boil, boil for 3 minutes, then simmer 30 minutes. Serves 8–10.

Editor's Extra: If you can't find frozen seasoning blend in the frozen vegetable section of your grocery store, you can make up your own mix of chopped onions, bell peppers, celery, and parsley.

Throw-It-In-The-Pot Gumbo Soup

No chopping. No mixing. Gumbo doesn't get any easier than this.

1 (16-ounce) package frozen gumbo mix
1 (12-ounce) package frozen seasoning blend
1 teaspoon Creole seasoning
4 cups chicken broth
1 (1-pound) package frozen claw crabmeat

Combine all ingredients except crabmeat in a saucepan; bring to a boil. Reduce heat, add crabmeat, and simmer 15–20 minutes. Serve over rice. Serves 4.

Editor's Extra: Frozen gumbo mix consists of chopped okra, celery, onions, and red bell peppers. Frozen seasoning blend is chopped onion, celery, red and green bell peppers, and parsley, and no freezer should be without it!

Simple Fish Chowder

1 (14½-ounce) can diced tomatoes
3 stalks celery, chopped
1 teaspoon dried oregano
1 teaspoon dried basil
½ pound frozen fish fillets, cut into chunks

Heat undrained tomatoes, celery, oregano, and basil to a boil over medium heat. Salt and pepper to taste. Add frozen fish fillets. Reduce heat, and cook 10–15 minutes, until fish is opaque and flaky. Thin with a little water, if needed. Serves 2–4.

Toucan Corn Chowder

You're only two cans away from homemade soup!

½ small onion, chopped
2 tablespoons butter
1 (8-ounce) can whole-kernel corn, drained
1 (16-ounce) can cream-style corn
4 pieces bacon, cooked, crumbled

In a medium saucepan, sauté onion in butter 3 minutes. Add remaining ingredients, salt and pepper to taste, then simmer 10 minutes. Serves 4.

Vegetable Chili Made Easy

1 small zucchini, diced
1 (28-ounce) can diced tomatoes, undrained
1 (16-ounce) jar black bean salsa
1 teaspoon chili powder
1½ cups shredded mild Cheddar cheese, divided

Combine zucchini, tomatoes, salsa, and chili powder in saucepan. Bring to a boil on medium-high heat; reduce heat; simmer 10 minutes, stirring occasionally.

Sprinkle about 2 tablespoons cheese in 4 soup bowls; top with chili. Sprinkle additional cheese on top. Serves 4.

Chili in Minutes

1 pound ground chuck
1 onion, chopped
1 envelope chili seasoning
1 (14½-ounce) can stewed tomatoes
2 (16-ounce) cans hot chili beans

Cook beef and onion together in a large skillet till meat is browned; drain. Stir in chili seasoning, tomatoes, and beans. Simmer about 30 minutes. Serves 4–6.

Chicken Chili Quick

4 boneless, skinless chicken breasts, broiled or grilled,
  chopped
1 package white chili seasoning (or regular chili)
1 (10-ounce) can diced Ro-Tel tomatoes, undrained
2 (16-ounce) cans white beans, undrained
1½ cups water

Mix all of the above in a large stockpot, bring to a boil, reduce heat to low, and simmer about an hour.

The exact month, day, or even the year of Jesus' birth cannot be exactly determined. Due to a mistaken calculation based on the Roman Calendar by Dionysius Exiguus, it was long held that Jesus was born in the year 1 BC, making the following year, AD 1, the first throughout which he was alive.

The nativity accounts in the Gospels of Matthew and Luke do not mention a date or time of year, but many scholars now estimate Jesus' birth to be around **5** BC. In addition, the account of the shepherds' activities in Luke suggest a spring or summer date for Jesus' birth.

The early Christian church did not celebrate Jesus' birth. It wasn't until A.D. 440 that the church officially proclaimed **December 25th** as the birth of Christ. This was not based on any religious evidence, but on a feast observed near the winter solstice.

Creamy Oyster Stew

1 quart oysters, reserve 2 cups liquor
½ stick butter
2 cups whipping cream
½ teaspoon pepper
½ teaspoon celery salt

Bring 1 cup reserved liquor to a boil for 5 minutes, then skim away foam. Add butter, cream, pepper, and celery salt. Stir until well blended, then remove from heat; set aside.

Heat remaining liquor with oysters just until edges of oysters curl, about 5 minutes. Drain, and add oysters to cream mixture. Heat almost to a boil, and serve steaming hot. May garnish with paprika, if desired.

Minestrone Plus Stew

2 pounds ground chuck
2 (14½-ounce) cans diced tomatoes
2 (15-ounce) cans Ranch Style beans
2 (19-ounce) cans minestrone soup
¾ teaspoon sugar

Brown beef over medium-high heat in a large saucepan. Drain excess grease. Reduce heat to medium, and stir in tomatoes, beans, soup, and sugar. Salt and pepper to taste Stir occasionally until heated through. Serves 8–10.

Fast
and
Fabulous

FIVE ★ STAR

Salads

Sweet Cabbage Slaw

1 head cabbage, finely shredded
1 onion, diced
1 tablespoon sugar
1 tablespoon rice wine vinegar
3–4 tablespoons mayonnaise

Mix all ingredients in large bowl with a lid; season to taste. Cover and refrigerate till ready to serve.

Fruity Coleslaw

2 medium red Delicious apples, peeled, grated
1 (1-pound) bag coleslaw mix
2 tablespoons cider vinegar
1 tablespoon sugar
½ cup mayonnaise

Combine apples, coleslaw mix, vinegar, sugar, and mayonnaise. Season with black pepper, if desired. Toss well. Chill till served.

Grilled Fruit Toss

½ medium pineapple, cored, cut into ½-inch slices
1 medium mango, cut into ½-inch-thick slices
4 cups torn salad greens
1 cup halved cherry tomatoes
⅓ cup balsamic vinaigrette dressing

Spray grill with nonstick cooking spray. Preheat to medium-high heat. Grill pineapple and mango 3 minutes on each side or until lightly browned. Cut grilled fruit into bite-size pieces. In large salad bowl, mix fruit, greens, and tomatoes; toss lightly. Drizzle with dressing just before serving.

Camembert and Pear Salad

2 (1-ounce) wedges Camembert cheese
3 tablespoons honey Dijon dressing, divided
2 tablespoons honey roasted peanuts, finely chopped
2 generous handfuls mixed baby salad greens
½ medium pear, peeled, cut into 8 slices

Preheat oven to 325°. In small zipper bag, toss cheese wedges with 1 teaspoon dressing and peanuts; shake to coat cheese with the peanuts. Place cheese on ungreased baking sheet. Reserve any peanuts still remaining in bag. Bake cheese about 8 minutes, or until cheese is slightly softened. In a bowl, toss greens with remaining dressing and reserved peanuts. Divide evenly between 2 salad plates. Arrange 4 pear slices on each salad, then top each with warm cheese wedge. Serves 2.

A Touch of Gold Carrot Salad

4 large or 6 small carrots
½ cup golden raisins
½ cup crushed pineapple
¼ cup mayonnaise
1½ teaspoons granulated sugar

Shred carrots into a bowl. Stir in raisins, pineapple, mayonnaise, and sugar. Refrigerate several hours before serving. Serves 6–8.

Interstate Highway 5 runs from San Diego, California, to Blaine, Washington.

Interstate 5 (abbreviated **I-5**) is the westernmost interstate highway in the continental United States. Its odd number indicates that it is a north-south highway. Its southernmost point is at the international border between the United States and Mexico in the San Diego community of San Ysidro, California. Its northernmost point is at the international border between the United States and Canada at the Peace Arch in Blaine, Washington.

The Chinese believe that the universe is composed of **five** elements. These elements figure heavily in Chinese astrology, and also in feng shui. Feng shui is the art of living in harmony with your physical surroundings. The environment must allow elements to nurture each other. The elements are:

- Wood (green)—creative, social, ethical, and generous.
- Fire (red)—active, strong, impulsive, and attractive. Fire can be warm and comforting, or destructive.
- Earth (yellow)—solid, reliable, stable, and patient.
- Metal (gold, silver, metallic)—power, money, success, and intensity. It can also be destructive.
- Water (blue, black)—flowing, traveling, learning, communicating, and influencing others. Water can be gentle or destructive.

Prize-Winning Carrot Salad

An outstanding combination of flavors.

1½ cups shredded carrots
¼ cup dried cranberries
¼ cup chopped pecans
3 tablespoons honey-mustard salad dressing
1 teaspoon sugar

Stir together carrots, cranberries, pecans, salad dressing, and sugar. Season with salt and pepper to taste. Toss well. Chill until serving time.

Fresh Veggie Salad

½ pound fresh green beans, trimmed
1 small crookneck squash, sliced
1 cup halved grape tomatoes
1 teaspoon Mrs. Dash Garlic and Herb Seasoning
¼ cup zesty Italian dressing

Snap green beans in half. Cook 2 minutes in boiling water; drain and allow to cool completely.

In salad bowl, layer green beans, squash, tomatoes, and seasoning. Toss ingredients with dressing just before serving.

Spinach Salad with Apple and Toasted Pecans

1 medium apple, thinly sliced
2 tablespoons chopped celery
2 tablespoons poppy seed dressing
3 cups baby spinach leaves
2 tablespoons broken toasted pecans

Combine apples, celery, and dressing; toss to coat. Refrigerate, covered, until serving time. Toss with spinach and pecans just before serving.

Spinach and Strawberry Salad

1 (16-ounce) bag baby spinach leaves
1 quart fresh strawberries, washed, hulled, sliced
12 cherry tomatoes
1 red onion, sliced
½ cup poppy seed dressing, or to taste

Toss spinach, strawberries, tomatoes, and onion in large salad bowl. Add dressing just before serving; mix thoroughly. Serves 6.

Pretty Poppy Seed Salad

Grapefruit and strawberries are a delicious combination in a salad. This is a beautiful and colorful presentation.

1 (10-ounce) bag spinach leaves, washed, dried
12 strawberries, stemmed, halved
1 pink grapefruit, peeled, sectioned
⅓ cup sliced almonds, toasted
½ cup poppy seed dressing

Arrange spinach leaves on 6 salad plates with strawberries and grapefruit sections on top. Sprinkle with almonds. Drizzle dressing over each salad right before serving.

Corn-On-The-Cob Salad

1 (7-ounce) bag torn mixed Italian greens
2 ears corn-on-the-cob, grilled, cooled, kernels
removed
10–12 cherry tomatoes, halved
⅓ cup zesty Italian dressing
¼ cup shredded Parmesan cheese

In large bowl, toss greens with corn and tomatoes. Add dressing; toss lightly. Sprinkle with cheese. Serves 4–6.

Touch of Green Waldorf Salad

1 large apple, peeled, chopped small
⅓ cup raisins
1 tablespoon chopped pecans
2 tablespoons mayonnaise
3 tablespoons snipped-small green lettuce

Mix all together; salt and pepper to taste. Serves 2–3.

Easy Caesar Salad

8 cups torn romaine lettuce
1 cup seasoned croutons
¼ cup bacon bits
⅓ cup shredded Parmesan cheese
⅔ cup Caesar salad dressing

Layer lettuce, croutons, bacon bits, and Parmesan in a large bowl. Right before serving, add dressing, and toss to coat.

Pretty French Salad

3 medium tomatoes
½ cup French dressing
1 small head lettuce
1 avocado
¼ cup crumbled Roquefort cheese

Wash and stem tomatoes and cut into eighths. Pour French dressing over tomatoes and let stand ½ hour.

Wash and drain lettuce, then tear leaves into small pieces. Peel and slice avocado into crescent slices. On 6 salad plates, arrange lettuce, then tomatoes, then avocado slices, then Roquefort cheese. Pour French dressing from marinated tomatoes over top before serving. Serves 6.

Sunflower Lentil Salad

10 cups torn mixed salad greens
1½ cups chopped tomatoes
1 cup cooked lentils (about ⅓ cup raw)
½ cup Italian salad dressing
¼ cup dry roasted sunflower seeds

Toss greens, tomatoes, and lentils with dressing. Garnish with sunflower seeds. Serves 8–10.

Basil Cream Tomatoes

¾ cup mayonnaise
⅓ cup half-and-half
1½ teaspoons chopped fresh basil, divided
4 medium tomatoes, sliced
½ medium red onion, sliced into thin rings

In a bowl with a lid, mix together mayonnaise, half-and-half, and ½ the basil. Cover and refrigerate until serving time. Just before serving, arrange tomatoes and onion on salad plates. Drizzle with dressing, and garnish with remaining basil. Serves 12.

"**Pente**" is the Greek word for **five**.

Pente is also the name of a board game created in 1978 by Gary Gabrel. Played with white and black marbles, the players alternate in placing stones of their color on free intersections. The players aim to create **five** vertically, horizontally, or diagonally connected stones of their color. The player who first creates **five** connected stones or captures **five** of the opponent's pairs wins.

Poseidon Salad

2 plum tomatoes, cut into wedges
1 medium cucumber, peeled, chopped
⅓ cup pitted kalamata olives, halved
¼ cup Greek vinaigrette dressing
⅓ cup crumbled feta cheese

Combine tomatoes, cucumbers, olives, and dressing in serving bowl. Toss to coat. Sprinkle with cheese just before serving.

Creamy Cucumber Salad

3 tablespoons sugar
¼ cup fresh lemon juice
1 (8-ounce) container sour cream
½ teaspoon dill weed
1 cucumber, peeled, seeded, sliced thinly

Whisk together sugar and lemon juice. When dissolved, stir in remaining ingredients. Season with salt and pepper to taste, if desired. Chill until served.

Cuke-&-Cado Salad

1½ cups julienned cucumber
1 ripe avocado, peeled, pitted, cubed
¼ cup diced purple onion
2 tablespoons chopped cilantro leaves
3 tablespoons zesty Italian dressing

Mix ingredients in medium salad bowl, tossing to coat. Season with salt and pepper to taste, if desired. Chill until serving time. Serves 4.

Fresh Broccoli Salad

3 cups chopped broccoli florets
⅓ cup chopped red onion
1 cup Mandarin oranges slices
¾ cup mayonnaise
3 tablespoons sugar

Mix broccoli, onion, and Mandarin oranges in a salad bowl. Combine mayonnaise and sugar. Toss with broccoli mixture. Cover and chill till serving time. Serves 4.

Red, White, and Broccoli Salad

1 (8-ounce) package seashell pasta
½ cup finely chopped cauliflower
½ cup finely chopped broccoli
½ cup diced red bell pepper
1¼ cups zesty Italian dressing

Cook pasta in a large pot of boiling salted water for about 10 minutes. Drain, and run under cold water to stop the cooking process. Combine cooled pasta, cauliflower, broccoli, red bell pepper, and salad dressing in a salad bowl. Season with salt and pepper to taste, if desired.

The **five**-pointed star is thought to have first appeared on August 3, 1777, on the flag of the newly declared United States of America at the site of the present city of Rome, New York.

George Washington's original pencil sketch for the flag indicated six-pointed stars, a form he apparently preferred.

Betsy Ross, however, recommended a **five-pointed** star. When the committee protested that it was too difficult to make, she took a piece of paper, folded it deftly, and with a single snip of her scissors, produced a symmetrical **five**-pointed star. This seeming feat of magic so impressed her audience that they readily agreed to her suggestion.

Marinated Roasted Pepper Salad

Good on a green salad, as a side dish, or all by itself.

1 large green bell pepper
1 large yellow bell pepper
1 large red bell pepper
1 tablespoon red wine vinegar
3 tablespoons olive oil

Preheat broiler. Place peppers on baking sheet in broiler and allow skins to blacken. Remove from oven and place in large zipper bag(s); seal. Allow to sit and steam about 20 minutes, then peel and seed peppers. Cut peppers into ½-inch-wide strips. In large salad bowl, combine peppers and vinegar. Season with salt and pepper to taste. Slowly stir in oil; mix well. Allow to stand at least 2 hours before serving at room temperature. Serves 4.

Editor's Extra: Experiment with different vinegar flavors for a twist on taste.

Asparagus Salad

3 tablespoons vegetable broth
3 tablespoons white wine vinegar
1 pound thin asparagus, trimmed and peeled
3 tablespoons chopped chives
3 tablespoons freshly grated Parmesan cheese

Bring broth and vinegar to a rolling boil in a large skillet. Place asparagus in boiling broth mixture, and cook 3–6 minutes, till tender-crisp. While asparagus cooks, fill a large bowl half full with ice, then add enough cold water to come up to top of ice. When asparagus spears are cooked, remove and immediately submerge them in the ice bath to cool completely. Drain and remove ice, then sprinkle with chives and cheese. Add pepper to taste, if desired. Keep chilled until serving time.

Tailgate Macaroni Salad

Good with anything!

1 (12-ounce) package small macaroni
1 dozen eggs, hard boiled, chopped
1 (15-ounce) can English peas, drained
1 cup Miracle Whip salad dressing
2 tablespoons minced sweet onion

Cook and drain macaroni. Put in salad bowl with remaining ingredients; season with salt and pepper to taste. Chill before serving. Serves 8–12.

Tri-Colored Pasta Salad

1 (16-ounce) package tri-colored pasta
2 cups diced tomatoes
1 cup finely chopped red onion
¾ cup peeled and diced cucumber
1 (16-ounce) bottle Italian salad dressing

Cook pasta in large pot of boiling salted water about 10 minutes. Drain, and run under cold water to stop the cooking process. Combine cooled pasta, tomatoes, onion, cucumber, and Italian dressing. Refrigerate at least 1 hour before serving. Season with salt and pepper to taste, if desired.

Got-It-Made Pasta Salad

1 Vidalia onion, chopped
½ stick butter
1 (12-ounce) package vermicelli, cooked, drained
2 medium tomatoes, cut small
1 (8-ounce) bottle Italian dressing

In large skillet, sauté onion in butter. Add pasta, tomatoes, and dressing. Toss well with tongs. Good warm or chilled.

Editor's Extra: Good to sauté fresh sliced mushrooms with the onion. Whole pitted black olives add a new dimension, too. And for extra color and flavor, toss in some chopped parsley.

Rotini Shrimp Salad

1 (16-ounce) package frozen carrots and snap peas
1 cup rotini pasta, cooked, drained
1 cup halved cherry tomatoes
½ pound shrimp, cooked
½ cup honey mustard salad dressing

Cook vegetables as directed on package; allow to cool. Mix all ingredients together and refrigerate for 1 hour before serving. Serves 6.

Creamy Mustard Dressing

¼ cup mustard
2 tablespoons sugar
2 tablespoons apple cider vinegar
2 tablespoons half-and-half
¼ teaspoon salt

Combine mustard, sugar, vinegar, half-and-half, and salt, and beat until creamy.

United Nations Salad Dressing

1 (16-ounce) bottle Thousand Island salad dressing
1 envelope Italian dressing mix
³⁄₄ cup sour cream
³⁄₄ cup mayonnaise
2 tablespoons soy sauce

Combine ingredients in mixing bowl and whisk together. Serve over green salad or shrimp salad.

Shrimp Cocktail Mold

1 (3-ounce) package lemon Jell-O
1 cup hot water
1 (4¼-ounce) can shrimp, drained
³⁄₄ cup cocktail sauce
½ cup chopped celery

Dissolve Jell-O in hot water. Add remaining ingredients. Transfer mixture to a lightly greased mold or loaf pan. Chill until set. Unmold onto salad greens, if desired.

Peachy Cream

Divine. Simply divine.

1 (12-ounce) container frozen whipped topping,
 thawed
1 (3-ounce) package peach Jell-O
1 (16-ounce) container sour cream
1 (15-ounce) can raspberry-flavored sliced peaches,
 cut small
1 (11-ounce) can Mandarin oranges, drained

Mix all together well. That's all there is to it. Refrigerate leftovers, if there are any.

The United Nations Security Council (UNSC) is charged with maintaining peace and security among nations. The Security Council is the only division of the United Nations that has the power to make decisions that member governments must carry out. The Security Council is made up of **fifteen** member states, consisting of **five** permanent seats and ten temporary seats. The permanent **five** are China, France, Russia, the United Kingdom, and the United States. These members hold veto power over substantive but not procedural resolutions.

The ten temporary seats are held for two-year terms with member states voted in by the UN General Assembly on a regional basis. The Presidency of the Security Council is rotated alphabetically each month.

Fluffy Fruit Salad

2 cups small curd cottage cheese
1 (12-ounce) container frozen Cool Whip, thawed
1 (11-ounce) can Mandarin oranges, drained
1 (8-ounce) can crushed pineapple, drained
1 (3-ounce) package lemon Jell-O

Stir together cottage cheese and Cool Whip. Add oranges and pineapple. Sprinkle with Jell-O and stir to combine well. Refrigerate until served.

Bing-O Salad

1 (16-ounce) can pitted Bing cherries, drained, juice reserved
1 (3-ounce) package lemon gelatin
1 cup sour cream
½ teaspoon almond extract
½ cup chopped pecans

Drain cherries; measure juice in a 4-cup measure, adding water, if necessary, to make 1 cup. Heat juice in microwave and dissolve gelatin in it. Chill till it begins to thicken; stir in sour cream and almond extract. Add cherries and nuts, and blend well. Pour into a lightly greased mold or loaf pan. Chill till set. Serve on a lettuce leaf, with a dab of mayonnaise, if desired.

5

A Cool Pear Salad

1 (15-ounce) can pears, drained (reserve syrup)
1 teaspoon lemon juice
1 (3-ounce) box lemon Jell-O
1 (3-ounce) package cream cheese, softened
1 cup whipping cream, whipped

Measure pear juice and lemon juice, adding water if needed to make 1 cup. Bring to a boil in medium saucepan. Remove from heat, add gelatin, and stir until completely dissolved. Allow to cool slightly. Mash pears. Gradually add cream cheese, and whisk until smooth. Fold cream cheese mixture and whipped cream into gelatin mixture. Pour into a lightly greased mold, and chill until set. Serves 12.

Light and Lovely Pineapple Apricot Salad

This can be a dessert—it's heavenly.

1 (6-ounce) package apricot gelatin
1 (16-ounce) can crushed pineapple, undrained
2 cups buttermilk
1 (8-ounce) carton frozen whipped topping, thawed
⅔ cup chopped pecans

Boil together gelatin and crushed pineapple. Allow to cool, then stir in buttermilk, whipped topping, and pecans. Pour into a large casserole and refrigerate till set.

Seafoam Salad

As cool as its color.

1 (3-ounce) package pistachio instant pudding mix
1 (12-ounce) tub frozen whipped topping, thawed
1 (20-ounce) can crushed pineapple, undrained
1½ cups miniature marshmallows
¾ cup chopped pecans

Fold dry pudding into whipped topping, then add pineapple, marshmallows, and pecans, and stir well. Chill till ready to serve. Serves 6–8.

Heath Apple Salad

Apple salad never tasted so good.

1 (8-ounce) package cream cheese, softened
½ cup brown sugar
4 Granny Smith apples, peeled, chopped
⅔ cup Heath Bites
3 cups frozen Cool Whip, thawed

Mix cream cheese and brown sugar well; add apples and Heath Bites. Fold in Cool Whip.

Frosted Fruit Salad

1 (8-ounce) can pineapple chunks, drained
2 bananas, sliced
1 (11-ounce) can Mandarin oranges, drained
1 cup halved purple grapes
1 (6-ounce) container lemon yogurt

In glass serving bowl, combine fruits; toss with yogurt till frosted. May serve immediately or refrigerate until serving time. Serves 4–6.

Frosted Grape Salad

Pretty in stemware for an elegant presentation.

1 cup packed brown sugar
1 cup sour cream
1 teaspoon almond extract
1 cup chopped pecans or almonds
2 cups seedless grapes (white and red)

Combine sugar, sour cream, and almond extract; fold in pecans. Cut grapes in half, if desired, and toss until well coated in sour cream mixture. Cover and refrigerate until serving time.

Editor's Extra: For a nice presentation, rather than tossing grapes in cream mixture, layer grapes, then sour cream mixture in stemmed glasses.

Banana Candlestick Salad

A fun salad that's a guaranteed conversation piece.

6 pineapple slices
2 bananas, peeled, cut in thirds
½ cup mayonnaise
¼ cup peanut butter
6 maraschino cherries

Place pineapple slices on 6 salad plates. Put flat end of banana into hole of pineapple (that's your candle). May need to taper top of bananas to resemble candles and/or trim bottoms to fit into pineapple holes. Combine mayonnaise and peanut butter and drizzle down bananas (that's your candle wax). Place cherries on top of each banana (that's your flame). Serves 6.

Short Circuit (1986) is a comedy sci-fi film starring Ally Sheedy and Steve Guttenberg, and a robot character called "**Johnny 5**."

The story revolves around an intelligent robot designated as **Number 5**—one of **five** prototype robots proposed for use by the U.S. military. A lightning storm creates a power surge that hits **Number 5** while it is recharging and alters its program, causing the robot to become peace-loving and capable of human feelings.

Developing human-like qualities, the robot later takes the name "**Johnny 5**."

Curried Pumpkin Seeds

2 cups fresh pumpkin seeds
1 tablespoon vegetable oil
2 teaspoons kosher salt
½ teaspoon curry powder
⅓ cup grated Parmesan cheese

Wash pumpkin seeds, removing any attached fibers. Soak seeds in salted water for 4 hours; drain.

Preheat oven to 350°. Place seeds and oil in a zipper bag, and seal. Rub bag to coat seeds. Bake seeds on jellyroll pan about 15 minutes, stirring occasionally. In another zipper bag, combine salt, curry powder, and cheese; add seeds and toss to coat evenly. Bake about 10 minutes longer, until crisp.

Fast
and
Fabulous

FIVE ★ STAR

Vegetables

Extra Special Baked Beans

1 cup chopped onion
1 pound hamburger meat, cooked, drained
4 (16-ounce) cans pork and beans
1 cup sweet barbecue sauce
¾ cup brown sugar

Preheat oven to 350°. Sauté onion, and brown meat together in skillet; drain. Combine meat and onion with beans, barbecue sauce, and brown sugar; stir well. Pour into a greased 9x13-inch casserole, and bake 50–60 minutes.

Cookout Baked Beans

4 (16-ounce) cans baked beans, drained
1 (12-ounce) bottle chili sauce
1 large onion, chopped
½ pound bacon, cooked, crumbled
2 cups packed brown sugar

Combine all ingredients and place in ungreased 3-quart baking dish. Bake uncovered in 325° oven 1 hour or until heated through and glazed. Serves 10–12.

Baked Butter Beans 'n Tomatoes

1 (16-ounce) package frozen butter beans, cooked
1 (14½-ounce) can diced tomatoes, drained
½ cup chopped onion
½ cup chopped green bell pepper
½ cup grated sharp Cheddar cheese, divided

In a large bowl, stir together butter beans, tomatoes, onion, pepper, and ½ the cheese, adding salt and pepper to taste. Place ingredients in a greased, 1½-quart baking dish. Sprinkle with remaining cheese. Bake 25–30 minutes or until bubbly. Serves 4.

Barbecued Italian Green Beans

A delightful veggie alternative for your cookout.

5 (14-ounce) cans Italian green beans, drained
1½ cups chopped onions
1 cup ketchup
1 cup packed brown sugar
6 slices bacon, diced

Preheat oven to 250°. Mix green beans, onions, ketchup, brown sugar, and bacon. Pour into an ungreased 9x13-inch casserole dish, and bake 2½–3 hours. Can also cook on LOW in crockpot for several hours.

Outstanding Green Bean Casserole

A great make-ahead, refrigerate, and reheat dish.

6 strips bacon
⅓ cup chopped onion
2 (10-ounce) packages frozen sliced green beans, cooked, drained
1 cup grated Cheddar cheese
1 (4-ounce) can sliced mushrooms, drained

Cook bacon in skillet till crisp; drain and crumble; reserve drippings. Sauté onion in bacon drippings until translucent. Add remaining ingredients to skillet, and cook over medium heat till cheese melts. Pour into 1½-quart casserole, and bake 20 minutes at 350°. Serves 6.

The **Five Principles** of Peaceful Coexistence are a series of agreements between the People's Republic of China and India. After the Central Chinese Government regained control of Tibet, China came into increasing conflict with India. In **1954**, the two nations drew up the **Five Principles** of Peaceful Coexistence:

1. Mutual respect for each other's territorial integrity and sovereignty
2. Mutual non-aggression
3. Mutual non-interference in each other's internal affairs
4. Equality and mutual benefit
5. Peaceful co-existence

As norms of relations between nations, these principles have become widely recognized and accepted throughout the world.

Cheese 'n Crackers Bean Casserole

2 (8-ounce) jars jalapeño Cheez Whiz
3 (16-ounce) cans French-style green beans, drained
1 (8-ounce) can sliced water chestnuts, drained, chopped
1½ cups crushed saltine crackers
¼ cup butter, melted

Preheat oven to 350°. In microwave, heat Cheez Whiz per instructions on jar. Pour into a greased baking dish. Add green beans and water chestnuts; stir well. Mix cracker crumbs with butter; sprinkle over top. Bake at 350° for 30 minutes. Serves 8.

Southern Pole Beans

Don't get in a hurry on this recipe; it's worth the wait.

2 pounds fresh pole beans, strings removed, ends trimmed, snapped 2 inches long
6 pieces bacon
1 tablespoon oil
1 cup strong chicken broth
3 tablespoons butter

Wash beans well, then drain. Fry bacon in cast-iron skillet or Dutch oven; reserve drippings, and set bacon aside. Sauté pole beans in hot bacon drippings and oil until bright green, about 5 minutes, turning occasionally. Add chicken broth, butter, and crumbled bacon. Add just enough water to almost cover the beans. Season with salt and pepper to taste. Bring to a boil, then lower heat to a simmer. Simmer several hours, until beans are very tender and slightly shriveled. Turn every 30 minutes or so, allowing beans on top to go to bottom. More water may have to be added during cooking to keep water level almost covering beans.

Good Ole Basic Fried Okra

½ cup cornmeal
½ teaspoon salt
¼ teaspoon pepper
1 pound fresh okra, cleaned, trimmed, sliced
¼ cup vegetable oil

Combine cornmeal, salt, and pepper. Add okra, and coat well. Heat oil till hot; fry okra in batches till browned, adding more oil if necessary. Drain on paper towels. Taste for seasoning.

Old Timey Corn Fritters

2 cups whole-kernel corn
3 eggs, beaten
2 tablespoons milk
1 tablespoon melted butter
About 1¼ cups self-rising flour

Process corn in food processor until slightly crushed. Mix together corn, eggs, milk, and melted butter, adding salt and pepper to taste. Add just enough flour to hold fritters together. Drop by tablespoons in hot oil, and cook 3–4 minutes, or until golden brown on both sides. Only fry a few at a time, so as not to crowd. Drain on paper towels, and serve hot.

The **five** most popular children's names in America (2005) are:

Boys:
1. Jacob
2. Michael
3. Joshua
4. Matthew
5. Ethan

Girls:
1. Emily
2. Emma
3. Madison
4. Abigail
5. Olivia

The **five** true vowels in the English alphabet are A, E, I, O, and U.

The longest word having only one vowel is "strengths."

The longest common word without any of the **five** vowels is "rhythms."

The word "abstemious" contains all **five** vowels—in alphabetical order—plus **five** consonants. It means "marked by restraint, especially in the consumption of food and drink."

Fried Field Corn

8–10 ears fresh corn on the cob
3 tablespoons butter
½ teaspoon salt
1½ tablespoons sugar
¼ cup water

Shuck corn and remove silks. With a sharp knife, cut only the tops of the corn kernels into a bowl. With corn tilted into bowl, scrape pulp from cob (using a spoon works best).

In a heavy skillet, melt butter, then add corn. Add salt, sugar, and water. Bring to a boil, then lower heat to medium. Cook until thickened, stirring often and adding more water, if needed.

"Fresh off the Cob" Corn

Well, it surely tastes authentic!

1 stick butter
3 (1-pound) bags frozen whole-kernel corn, thawed, divided
2 cups half-and-half
1½ teaspoons salt
1½ teaspoons pepper

Melt butter in a heavy skillet. Pour 1 bag corn into a blender with half-and-half. Purée and pour into skillet with remaining 2 bags corn. Add salt and pepper. Stir constantly and bring to a boil. Reduce heat to medium low and cook covered, stirring frequently, for 15–20 minutes. Uncover and cook an additional 15–20 minutes, still stirring frequently.

Easy Corn Pudding

2 (15-ounce) cans cream-style corn
½ cup milk
⅓ cup sugar
2 eggs, well beaten
½ stick butter

Preheat oven to 375°. Mix all ingredients except butter, and pour into greased baking pan. Cut butter into pats, and place on top. Season with salt and pepper to taste. Bake 45–60 minutes, until pudding is firm to the touch.

Corn 'n Green Chiles Casserole

¾ (8-ounce) package cream cheese
2 tablespoons butter
1 (4-ounce) can chopped green chiles
Dash of garlic salt
2 (15-ounce) cans shoe peg corn

Melt cream cheese and butter in saucepan. Stir in remaining ingredients. Pour into a greased casserole and bake in 350° oven until heated through, about 20 minutes.

Gotta-Try-It Hominy Casserole

2 (15-ounce) cans hominy
1 (4-ounce) can diced green chiles
⅓ cup chopped green onions
1 (8-ounce) carton sour cream
½ cup shredded Cheddar cheese

Preheat oven to 350°. Drain 1 can hominy, then blend with remaining ingredients except cheese. Pour into a greased 2-quart casserole. Sprinkle cheese over top. Bake for 35 minutes.

Flavorful Broccoli and Corn Casserole

1 (10-ounce) package frozen chopped broccoli
25 seasoned crackers
1 stick butter, melted
1 (15-ounce) can whole-kernel corn
1 (15-ounce) can cream-style corn

Cook broccoli as directed on package. Crumble crackers and mix with butter; reserve 1 cup. Mix broccoli, corns, and crackers; place in greased 2-quart casserole dish. Sprinkle reserved crackers over mixture; heat at 350° for 20 minutes or until hot.

Mediterranean Broccoli

Different . . . easy . . . delicious!

2 (10-ounce) packages frozen broccoli spears, cooked,
**   drained**
2 tablespoons butter or margarine
¼ cup cider vinegar
½ cup French dressing
⅓ cup sliced pimento-stuffed olives

Gently mix together hot broccoli, butter, vinegar, and French dressing; fold in olives. Serve warm. Serves 6–8.

Broccoli Cheese Casserole

1 egg, beaten
1 cup mayonnaise
1 (10¾-ounce) can cream of mushroom soup
1 cup shredded Cheddar cheese
2 (10-ounce) boxes frozen chopped broccoli, thawed,
**   drained**

Preheat oven to 350°. Mix egg, mayonnaise, cream of mushroom soup, cheese, and broccoli. Pour into a greased 1½-quart casserole. Bake at 350° for 30 minutes.

Broccoli Puff Casserole

2 bunches broccoli, cut into spears
2 egg whites, room temperature
¼ teaspoon salt
½ cup shredded Swiss cheese
½ cup mayonnaise

Cook and drain broccoli spears. Put in lightly greased broiler-proof serving dish or pan. Beat egg whites and salt until stiff peaks form. Fold in cheese and mayonnaise; spoon evenly over broccoli. Broil 6 inches from heat for 4 minutes or until golden brown. Serve hot. Serves 6–8.

Easy Eggs Florentine

1 (10¾-ounce) can cream of celery soup
¼ cup milk
2 (10-ounce) packages frozen chopped spinach,
   cooked, drained
5 eggs, beaten
1 cup cubed Velveeta

Combine soup, milk, and spinach. Add salt and pepper to taste. Spread in bottom of greased 2-quart baking dish. Top with beaten eggs. Sprinkle with cheese cubes. Bake at 350° about 30 minutes or until eggs are set. Serves 6.

What's so special about the **5th** of April 2006? At 1:02 am and 3 seconds on Wednesday, April **5**, 2006, it was the 1st hour of the day, the 2nd minute of the hour, the 3rd second of that minute in the 4th month and the **5th** day of 2006 . . . or just 01:02:03 04-05-06 for short!

Red Cabbage and Apple Braise

2 tablespoons canola oil
1 cup chopped Granny Smith apple
2 cups apple juice
½ teaspoon caraway seeds
1 small red cabbage, shredded

Heat large skillet; add canola oil. Braise apple for 1 minute, then add apple juice and caraway seeds. Add cabbage; stir slightly to coat. Reduce heat, cover, and cook 25 minutes. Salt to taste.

Editor's Extra: You can add a pat of butter and a squeeze of lemon to harmonize the flavors further.

Saucy Eggplant Mozzarella

1 eggplant, peeled, sliced
½ cup flour
½ cup canola oil
1 (26-ounce) jar spaghetti sauce
2½ cups shredded mozzarella cheese

Coat eggplant with flour. Heat oil in skillet, and brown eggplant on both sides; drain on paper towels. In a large baking dish, layer ½ the eggplant, ½ the spaghetti sauce, and ½ the cheese. Sprinkle with salt and pepper to taste. Repeat layers. Cover with foil, and bake at 350° for 35 minutes.

Easy Italian Eggplant Parmigiana

1 large eggplant, peeled
½ stick butter, melted
¾–1 cup seasoned Italian bread crumbs
1 (16-ounce) jar seasoned spaghetti sauce
4–6 slices mozzarella cheese

Cut eggplant into ½-inch slices. Dip slices in butter, then bread crumbs. Place on nonstick baking sheet. Spoon spaghetti sauce on each slice. Top eggplant with cheese slices, cutting to distribute evenly. Bake in 400° oven 15–20 minutes or until cheese is slightly brown. Serves 6.

Sweet Georgia Brown

1 onion, chopped
2 tablespoons vegetable oil
1 eggplant, peeled, cubed small
2 cups chopped tomatoes
1 tablespoon brown sugar

In 10-inch skillet over medium heat, sauté onion in oil. Stir in eggplant, tomatoes, and sugar. Reduce heat to low and simmer until eggplant and tomatoes are tender, about 15 minutes. Season to taste. Serves 6.

Deep-Fried Eggplant

2 medium eggplants, peeled, sliced ½ inch thick
1–2 teaspoons salt
1 egg, beaten
½ cup milk
2 cups plain bread crumbs

Sprinkle eggplant slices with salt; place in a colander, and allow to sit and drain at room temperature for 20–30 minutes. Rinse, and pat dry. In a shallow bowl, combine egg with milk. Place bread crumbs in a separate shallow bowl. Season crumbs with salt and pepper to taste. Dip eggplant into egg-milk mixture, then coat with seasoned bread crumbs. Deep-fry in hot oil 3–4 minutes, until golden brown on both sides. Serve hot.

Sweet Tomato Pudding

1 cup tomato purée
1 cup brown sugar
¼ cup water
2 cups dry bread cubes, crusts removed
½ cup butter, melted

Combine tomato purée, brown sugar, and water, and cook 5 minutes. Put bread cubes in a greased casserole, and pour melted butter over. Pour hot tomato mixture over all. Do not stir. Bake 50 minutes in a 325° oven. Serves 6.

Editor's Extra: Best to cut crust from bread, cube it small, then let sit out till very dry. This gives the pudding a nice crusty texture.

Fried Green Tomatoes

2 eggs, beaten
1 cup buttermilk
1 cup self-rising flour
1 teaspoon salt
2 large green tomatoes, sliced ¼ inch thick

In a shallow bowl, mix eggs with buttermilk. In another bowl, mix flour and salt; add pepper to taste. Dip tomato slices in egg-milk mixture, then coat with seasoned flour. Without crowding, fry in 1 inch of hot oil 3–4 minutes, or till golden brown and crisp on both sides. Sprinkle lightly with salt as soon as you remove from oil, then drain on paper towels. Serve hot.

Spruced-Up Canned Veggies

2 (15-ounce) cans Veg-All, drained
1 cup shredded Cheddar cheese
¾ cup mayonnaise
1 stick butter, melted
1 sleeve Ritz Crackers, crushed

Preheat oven to 350°. Mix Veg-All, cheese, mayonnaise, and butter, and pour into a buttered casserole dish. Sprinkle Ritz crumbs over top. Bake about 30 minutes, or till thoroughly heated.

It is generally believed that humans have **five** senses that help them interact with others and get around in their daily lives. Those **five** senses are sight, smell, hearing, taste, and touch—classifications first devised by Aristotle.

Some animals have senses that humans do not, including:

- Magnetoception: the ability to detect fluctuations in magnetic fields. This can be observed in birds and bees, and seems to be essential to their navigational abilities, but it is not well-understood.

- Electroreception: the ability to receive and make use of electrical impulses, mainly to locate an object. It is most common among aquatic creatures.

- Echolocation: the ability to determine orientation to other objects through interpretation of reflected sound. Bats are noted for this ability, awhich is used to navigate through the dark.

Mexi-Veggie Bake

Creating a meal at the Quail Ridge Press office is always interesting, especially when using whatever you find in the communal frig/freezer. This was a definite hit.

**½ (32-ounce) bag frozen shredded hash brown
   potatoes**
1 (4-ounce) can diced green chiles
**1 (19-ounce) bag frozen broccoli/cauliflower mix
   with garlic herb seasoning**
½ (1-pound) block Mexican Velveeta
¼ stick butter

Place hash browns and green chiles in greased 2-quart casserole dish. Thaw broccoli/cauliflower mix in microwave; add to hash brown mixture. Cut Velveeta into chunks; add to mixture along with pats of butter. Toss to distribute. Bake in 350° oven 20–25 minutes, until cheese is melted and mixture is bubbly.

Potatoes in Buttery Cream Sauce

I like to serve this cream sauce over hot cornbread.

4–6 medium potatoes, peeled, cut into chunks
½–1 stick butter
½ teaspoon salt
1–2 tablespoons cornstarch
⅛ cup milk

Boil potatoes in water to cover until tender, but not overcooked. Do not drain. Add butter and salt. Dissolve cornstarch in milk, and add slowly to simmering potatoes in water, stirring until desired thickness is achieved. Season with pepper to taste.

Editor's Extra: Parsley flakes may be sprinkled over finished dish for added flavor and eye appeal.

Cheesy Potato Hot Dish

1 (32-ounce) package frozen hash browns or O'Brien potatoes, thawed
1 stick butter, melted
1 (16-ounce) carton sour cream
1 (10¾-ounce) can cream of mushroom soup
2 cups shredded Cheddar cheese, divided

Combine all ingredients; mix well. Place in greased casserole dish and bake at 350° for 1 hour.

Micro Nacho Potatoes

2 medium gold potatoes
2 tablespoons thinly sliced green onions
2 tablespoons finely chopped green bell pepper
¼ cup taco sauce
⅓ cup shredded Mexican blend cheese

Scrub but don't peel potatoes. Cut into ⅜-inch slices. Arrange potato slices in a microwave-safe baking dish, putting smaller slices in the middle. Distribute green onions and green pepper. Cover and cook on HIGH 7–10 minutes or until tender, turning dish during cooking. Drizzle taco sauce over slices, then sprinkle with shredded cheese. Cook, uncovered, 45 seconds more or until cheese is melted. Serves 4.

Months of the year that begin on a Sunday always have **five** Sundays (other than February in non-leap years).

In order for there to be **five** Sundays in February, two things must happen. First, it must be a leap year. Second, February 1st must fall on a Sunday, so that the remaining four Sundays will fall on the 8th, 15th, 22nd, and 29th. The occurance of **five** Sundays in February happens 13 times in every 400-year span. The most recent occurance was in 2004. Future occurances in the next 400 years will happen in: 2032, 2060, 2088, 2128, 2156, 2184, 2224, 2252, 2280, 2320, 2348, and 2376.

Quick Homemade Mashed Potatoes for Two

1 huge Idaho potato, peeled, diced
2 tablespoons butter
3 tablespoons milk
½ teaspoon salt
¼ cup shredded Cheddar cheese, divided

Microwave diced potato in small casserole dish on HIGH in ⅓ cup water, covered, for 5 minutes. Let sit a minute, mash some, then add butter, milk, and salt. Microwave on HIGH another 2–3 minutes, till potatoes are soft. Mash completely. Divide onto 2 plates, making an indent in the middle. Evenly sprinkle cheese over each.

Flavorful Garlic Mashed Potatoes

4 medium potatoes, peeled, quartered
4 cups chicken stock
1 teaspoon minced garlic
½ cup butter
½ cup half-and-half

Boil potatoes in chicken stock with garlic. Bring to a boil, then reduce heat, and simmer until potatoes are soft; drain. Mash potatoes with butter and half-and-half. Salt and pepper to taste. Serves 4.

Sunburned Potato Bites

8–10 small potatoes, peeled
3 tablespoons bacon drippings
½ cup cornflake crumbs
2 teaspoons paprika
1 teaspoon salt

Preheat oven to 425°. Brush potatoes with bacon drippings. Roll in mixture of cornflake crumbs, paprika, and salt. Place in greased baking pan and bake 40 minutes till fork-tender.

Tastes Great Potatoes

So tasty, you may not get away with just plain potatoes ever again.

4 red potatoes, peeled, diced
1 generous teaspoon chicken soup base
⅓ cup frozen seasoning blend
½ teaspoon minced garlic
3–4 tablespoons butter

Boil potatoes with soup base, seasoning blend, and garlic in water to barely cover. Allow to boil slowly till water has almost completely evaporated, and potatoes are soft, 15–20 minutes. They are mashable now, but you can fold the butter in gently if you want to keep the potatoes in pieces. Taste to see if it needs more butter, and/or salt and pepper.

Editor's Extra: If you can't find frozen seasoning blend in the frozen vegetable section of your grocery store, you can make up your own mix of chopped onions, bell peppers, celery, and parsley.

Crunchy Cheesy Potatoes

⅓ cup butter
3 baking potatoes, peeled, sliced
¾ cup crushed cornflakes
1½ cups shredded Cheddar cheese
1½ teaspoons paprika

Melt butter in an 8x8-inch baking pan at 375°. Add sliced potatoes, turning in butter to coat. Mix remaining ingredients together, and sprinkle over potatoes. Bake 30 minutes, or until fork- tender. Serves 4–6.

Potatoes Done Light

4 small gold potatoes, peeled, diced
½ cup water
⅓ cup chopped onion
3 tablespoons Smart Balance Buttery Spread
1½ teaspoons Mrs. Dash Onion & Herb Seasoning

Put potatoes in 1½-quart baking dish with water. Cover and microwave on HIGH 6 minutes. Add onion, butter, and seasoning, adding salt and pepper to taste. Stir, re-cover, and microwave on HIGH another 5 minutes. Let sit another 3 minutes. Stir and serve. Serves 3–4.

Sour Cream Potatoes

4 potatoes, peeled, sliced
1 cup sour cream
1 envelope onion soup mix
1 teaspoon Greek seasoning
¼ cup half-and-half

Put potato slices in greased 2-quart baking dish. Mix remaining ingredients and spoon over potatoes. Cover securely with foil. Bake at 350° for 30–35 minutes. Serves 6.

French Onion Dip Potatoes

Make this a day ahead and it's even better.

8 medium potatoes, peeled, cubed, boiled
1 (8-ounce) package cream cheese, softened
1 (8-ounce) container French onion dip
½ teaspoon salt
½ stick butter

Mix drained potatoes, cream cheese, onion dip, and salt, and spoon into a greased 3-quart casserole dish; dot with butter. Bake covered at 350° for 35–40 minutes, a little longer if refrigerated overnight. Serves 8–10.

Cheddar Baked Potatoes

8 medium potatoes, baked
2 tablespoons butter or margarine
1 (10¾-ounce) can Cheddar cheese soup
1 tablespoon chopped chives
¼ teaspoon paprika

Cut baked potatoes in half lengthwise; scoop out insides, leaving a thin shell. With electric mixer, mash potatoes with butter. Gradually add soup and chives; beat until fluffy. Spoon into shells. Sprinkle with paprika. Bake in a 9x13-inch baking dish at 450° for 15 minutes Serves 8.

Editor's Extra: About potatoes: Russets are good for French fries or baked potatoes. Yellow Finn and Yukon Gold bake well, and micro-bake well, too. These roast good and make good scalloped potatoes. The reds and round whites, or new potatoes, boil good and make the best potato salad.

What **15**-letter word contains the letter "E" **five** times and no other vowels?

Answer: Defenselessness

Sweet Potato Skillet

This whole process takes less than fifteen minutes, and the results are Thanksgiving-table good!

1 (28-ounce) can sweet potatoes
3 tablespoons butter
1 teaspoon lemon juice
3 tablespoons brown sugar
1 cup mini marshmallows

Set oven to broil. Pour entire can of sweet potatoes into an oven-proof skillet and heat to boiling on stove top. Add butter, lemon juice, brown sugar, and salt and pepper to taste. Stir and mash till well mixed. Smooth potatoes in skillet and scatter marshmallows evenly over top. Broil 6 inches from heat only a minute or 2, watching till marshmallows brown on top. Serves 6.

Sweet Potato Sunset

4 small sweet potatoes, baked
1 cup brown sugar
1 (8-ounce) can crushed pineapple, drained
1 stick butter, melted
¾ cup shredded coconut

Preheat oven to 350°. Peel sweet potatoes, and place in a greased casserole dish; mash with a fork. Sprinkle with brown sugar and pineapple. Drizzle with butter, then top with coconut. Bake for 35 minutes.

Sweet Potato Praline Casserole

4 large sweet potatoes, baked
1 stick butter
⅓ cup packed brown sugar
2 eggs, beaten
½ cup chopped pecans

Peel sweet potatoes while still very warm, almost hot. Mash with butter in large mixing bowl. Add brown sugar and eggs, and mix well. Pour into a greased 2-quart baking dish, and top with pecans. Bake at 350° about 30 minutes.

Sweet Orange Beets

1 (16-ounce) can cut beets
1 tablespoon butter
2 teaspoons flour
2 tablespoons brown sugar
½ cup orange juice

In a small saucepan, heat beets in their liquid. In another small saucepan, melt butter. Quickly stir in flour, brown sugar, and orange juice. Heat, stirring constantly, until thickened. Drain beets and add to sauce. Heat and serve. Serves 4.

Standard **five-card draw** is often the first poker variant learned by most players, and is very common in home games, but rarely played in casinos or tournaments. Each player is dealt **five** cards, one at a time, all face down. Players look at their hand, and the first betting round occurs. Each player specifies how many of his cards he wishes to replace, and is dealt the same number of cards he discarded, so that each player again has **five** cards. A second betting round occurs, and the player with the best hand wins the pot.

Five-card stud, another form of poker, originated during the Civil War. Each player is dealt one card face down, followed by one card face up. After the first betting round is complete, another face-up card is dealt to each player. Subsequent betting rounds occur with an additional card added, until all players have **five** cards on the table. The best hand wins the pot.

A **quincunx** is an arrangement of **five** objects in a square— one at each corner and one in the middle (as the dots seen on the **5th** side of dice or dominoes).

A **quincunx** is a standard pattern for planting an orchard, especially in France.

Tasty, Good-For-You Sesame Carrots

The sesame seeds give such a tasty punch to carrots in this easy recipe. And it's so pretty.

1 teaspoon sesame seeds
2 pounds carrots, peeled, sliced
2 tablespoons brown sugar
Scant teaspoon lemon pepper
2–3 tablespoons butter

In a small skillet, toast sesame seeds for 2 minutes or so, just till seeds begin to turn golden brown. Put carrots into casserole dish with just enough water to cover bottom ($\frac{1}{3}$ cup or so). Sprinkle with sugar and lemon pepper, then put thin pats of butter all over. Cover and microwave on HIGH 9 minutes, stirring once or twice. Stir in sesame seeds, and cook 2 more minutes on HIGH. Let stand another 5 minutes. Serves 8–10.

Editor's Extra: Great colorful dish! You can use no-sodium lemon pepper and unsalted butter, and/or Splenda to reduce the already small amounts of sodium and sugar in this recipe, if your diet requests. But it's so yummy, you'll make it all the time for everybody!

Colorful Summer Sauté

A favorite when fresh vegetables are abundant.

2 tablespoons butter
2 tablespoons fresh chopped basil or pesto
2 cups sliced yellow squash
2 cups sliced zucchini
1 red bell pepper, sliced

In large skillet, melt butter and add basil or pesto, stirring well. Add yellow squash, zucchini, and red pepper, and toss well to coat. Cover and cook on medium heat 5 minutes, or until vegetables are tender. Makes 4 servings.

Sunday Squash Casserole

3 cups sliced yellow squash
1 cup chopped onion
1 (10¾-ounce) can cream of chicken soup
1 cup sour cream
1 cup buttered bread crumbs

Cook squash and onion in saucepan with a little water till tender; drain. Preheat oven to 350°. Mix squash, onion, soup, and sour cream, and pour into a greased 2-quart baking dish. Sprinkle with bread crumbs; bake 45 minutes. Serves 6.

Saucy Squash Dressing

2 cups crumbled prepared Mexican cornbread
4 medium yellow squash, sliced, cooked, drained
1 large onion, chopped
2 tablespoons butter, melted
1 (10¾-ounce) can nacho cheese soup

Crumble cornbread, and add to mashed squash; stir in onion, butter, and soup. Pour into greased 2-quart casserole; bake in 350° oven 35–40 minutes. Serves 6–8.

Greek Squash and Onion

1 squash, cut into chunks
1 sweet onion, split and quartered
4 tablespoons butter
1 teaspoon Greek seasoning
Sprinkle of basil

Place squash and onion in microwave-safe dish with lid. Put pats of butter on top; sprinkle with seasoning and basil. Cover and microwave on HIGH 3 minutes; toss and microwave another 1–2 minutes, till tender-crisp. Let set 2–3 minutes before serving. Serves 2.

Cheesy Baked Vidalias

5 Vidalia onions, peeled
⅓ cup water
½ cup crushed croutons
1 stick butter, melted
½ cup shredded Cheddar cheese

Quarter each onion, cutting only ⅔ of the way through. Put onions in a baking dish with water. Sprinkle with crushed croutons. Season with salt and pepper to taste. Pour melted butter over onions, making sure to let it sink down into the onion. Bake uncovered in 350° oven about 30 minutes, until tender. Top with Cheddar cheese; return to oven until melted. Serves 5.

Mexi-Stuffed Peppers

6 green bell peppers
1 cup prepared rice
1 (16-ounce) can red kidney beans, drained, rinsed
1 (16-ounce) can whole-kernel corn, undrained
1 envelope taco seasoning mix

Cut ½ inch off top of each pepper; remove seeds and veins; wash. Blanch in boiling water 5 minutes; drain. Place peppers in lightly greased baking dish. Combine rice with beans, corn, and taco seasoning. Stuff peppers, and bake uncovered at 350° for 25–30 minutes, or until heated through and slightly brown on top.

Old-Fashioned Stuffed Bell Peppers

4 bell peppers, all colors, if desired
1 pound ground beef
1 cup frozen seasoning blend
½ (5-ounce) can tomato sauce
1 cup cooked rice

Core and seed bell peppers; cut in half, and boil in water until tender, about 5 minutes. Drain; set aside.

In skillet on medium-high heat, sauté ground beef and seasoning blend. When meat is slightly brown and tender, add tomato sauce and rice. Simmer about 15 minutes. Put about ½ cup meat mixture in each pepper half. Top with a thin strip of pepper, for color. Place in casserole or pan large enough to hold peppers with about ½ inch of water in bottom of pan. Cook in 350° oven 25–30 minutes. Serves 6–8.

Editor's Extra: If you can't find frozen seasoning blend in the frozen vegetable section of your grocery store, you can make up your own mix of chopped onions, bell peppers, celery, and parsley.

Gwen's Baked Apples

I love to serve this with an all-vegetable meal and cornbread.

3 large green apples, peeled, sliced
3 tablespoons lemon juice
⅔ cup brown sugar
12 Ritz Crackers, crumbled
½ stick butter

Preheat oven to 375°. Place apple slices in small casserole dish. Sprinkle lemon juice over apples, then sugar, then cracker crumbs. Put thin pats of butter all over top. Bake 40 minutes (26 minutes covered; 15 minutes uncovered).

Editor's Extra: Easy to do in a toaster oven.

Citizen Kane (1941), Casablanca (1942), *The Godfather* (1972), *Gone with the Wind* (1939), and *Lawrence of Arabia* (1962) complete the top **five** movies of the American Film Institute's 100 greatest American movies of all time.

Five Spielberg films make the top 100:

#9 *Schindler's List* (1993)
#25 *E.T. the Extra-Terrestrial* (1982)
#48 *Jaws* (1975)
#60 *Raiders of the Lost Ark* (1981)
#64 *Close Encounters of the Third Kind* (1977)

Stove-Top Baked Apples

Good for breakfast, dessert, or as a side dish with meats.

1 cup water
2 tablespoons butter
1/2 cup sugar
1/8 teaspoon salt
2 firm green apples, unpeeled, quartered

In medium skillet, combine water, butter, sugar, and salt. Heat until boiling; boil 2 minutes before gently putting apple wedges in, skin side down. Continue cooking apples, dipping liquid over apples as they cook. Turn occasionally. Cook until apples are tender and juice has thickened, 5–8 minutes. May add a dash of cinnamon, if desired.

Favorite Apricot Side Dish

1 (29-ounce) can peeled apricots
3 tablespoons lemon juice
1/2 (1-pound) box light brown sugar
1/2 box Cheese Ritz Crackers
1/2 stick butter or margarine

Cut apricots in half, remove seeds, and drain for at least an hour. Turn cut side up in glass baking dish and sprinkle with lemon juice and sugar; marinate overnight in refrigerator.

Just before cooking, crumble crackers coarsely over apricots; drizzle with butter. Bake at 350° for 40–50 minutes. Serves 8.

Cheesy White Sauce for Baked Potatoes

1 stick butter, melted
1 cup mayonnaise
½ cup Parmesan cheese
¼ cup grated onion
1 teaspoon Worcestershire

Mix all ingredients together well. If sauce is too thin, add more cheese. Serve over hot baked potatoes. Fabulous!

Buttery Blender Hollandaise

Great over asparagus, broccoli, fish, grilled tomatoes, sandwiches, and eggs.

4 egg yolks
2–3 tablespoons fresh lemon juice
¼ teaspoon salt
Dash of pepper
1 stick butter, melted

Put egg yolks, lemon juice, salt, and pepper in blender. Pulse a few times, then turn to high speed and slowly add melted butter in a very thin but steady stream. Serve immediately over broccoli, asparagus, or grilled tomatoes.

Lemony Sauce to Liven-Up Vegetables

1 cup sour cream
¼ cup mayonnaise
2 tablespoons lemon juice
½ teaspoon salt
¼ teaspoon Tabasco

Whisk all ingredients together in a saucepan; heat, but do not boil. Makes enough sauce for 4–6 servings.

Editor's Extra: This is a great enhancement for most all vegetables. Spoon it on when serving, or offer at table, or put on top of vegetables in a casserole. Then add some bread crumbs or fried onion rings on top before broiling until brown.

Delmonico Delicious Sauce

⅔ cup plain French dressing
1 tablespoon tomato catsup
1½ teaspoons Worcestershire
1 tablespoon finely chopped green peppers
1 hard-boiled egg, very finely chopped, or rubbed through a sieve

Whisk together and serve on green vegetables or a salad.

Fast
and
Fabulous

FIVE ★ STAR

Pasta, Rice, Etc.

Oh-Zo Delicious Pasta

2 tablespoons olive oil
2 cloves garlic, minced
½ small onion, finely chopped
2 (14-ounce) cans chicken broth
2 cups uncooked orzo pasta

Place a saucepan over medium heat; when hot, pour in olive oil. Add garlic and onion; cook and stir about 3 minutes until tender. Pour in chicken broth, and stir and scrape the bottom of pan.

When broth boils, stir in orzo. Reduce heat to low, cover, and simmer 15 minutes, or until pasta has absorbed all liquid. Stir occasionally to prevent sticking. Season with salt and pepper before serving.

Red Haired Angel

1 (28-ounce) jar marinara sauce
1 (4-ounce) can chopped black olives
2 tablespoons capers, drained
½ teaspoon hot red pepper flakes (or to taste)
1 (8-ounce) package angel hair pasta, cooked, drained

In a small saucepan over medium-high heat, combine marinara sauce, olives, capers, and red pepper flakes. Bring to a boil, stirring occasionally, then remove from heat. To serve, spoon over angel hair pasta. May garnish with fresh basil or parsley. Garnish with Parmesan cheese. Serves 4.

Really Creamy Fettuccine

1 pound fettuccine
1 tablespoon lemon juice
½ pound Gorgonzola cheese
2 tablespoons unsalted butter
1 cup whipping cream

Cook pasta in boiling water according to package directions, adding lemon juice to boiling water; drain. Meanwhile, melt cut-up cheese and butter in top of double boiler over simmering water, whisking occasionally. Stir in cream, and remove from heat; allow to thicken. Toss pasta with sauce. Serves 6–8.

Editor's Extra: Sprinkle crushed basil leaves over the top for extra color and flavor.

Vegetable Pasta Toss

1 (8-ounce) package penne pasta
½ cup frozen green peas
½ cup asparagus tips
4 ounces Gorgonzola cheese
½ cup heavy whipping cream

Cook pasta in lightly salted boiling water with peas and asparagus. Cook 6 minutes, or until pasta is as you like it; drain.

Crumble cheese into cream; season with salt and pepper to taste. In large bowl, toss pasta and vegetables with cheese mixture until cheese has melted and pasta is well coated with sauce. Serve immediately. Serves 8.

"**Take Five**" is a classic jazz piece recorded by Dave Brubeck Quartet and released on the 1959 album *Time Out*. Composed by Paul Desmond, the group's saxophonist, the song became famous for its distinctive, catchy saxophone melody and use of **quintuple** time (**5** beats per measure), from which the piece gets its name. While "**Take Five**" was not the first jazz composition to use this unusual meter, it was the first of mainstream significance in the United States, becoming a hit at a time when rock music was in fashion.

The song has been covered by numerous artists, including a version with lyrics sung by Al Jarreau in 1977.

Recordings of "**Take Five**" have often been used in movies, including *Constantine* and *Pleasantville*.

Take five is also slang for "take a break."

In geometry, a **pentagon** is any **five**-sided polygon. However, the term is commonly used to mean a regular **pentagon**, where all sides are equal and all angles are equal (to 108°).

Buttery Italian Noodles

1 (8-ounce) package egg noodles
½–1 envelope dry Italian dressing mix
½ cup half-and-half
½ stick butter
¼ cup grated fresh Parmesan cheese

Cook noodles per package directions; drain well. Add remaining ingredients, and toss to blend. Serves 4.

Broccoli Vermicelli

1 (12-ounce) package vermicelli
4 cups broccoli florets, cut bite-size
2 tablespoons butter, sliced
12 slices bacon, cooked crisp, crumbled
¾ cup freshly grated Parmesan cheese, divided

Cook pasta in lightly salted boiling water according to package directions; drain, reserving ½ cup pasta water. Meanwhile, cook broccoli till tender-crisp. Combine hot broccoli and pasta; add butter, reserved pasta water, bacon, and Parmesan. Season with salt and freshly ground black pepper to taste. Toss well. Serves 8.

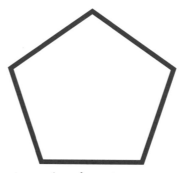

A regular pentagon

Trees and Butterflies

Okay, it's really broccoli and bowtie pasta, but just as good a combo.

1 (1-pound) package dry farfalle (bow tie) pasta
4 cups broccoli florets, cut small
4 cloves garlic, sliced
¼ cup olive oil, divided
1 cup grated Romano cheese

Boil farfalle pasta in lightly salted water for 8–10 minutes, until al dente. Drain, reserving ¼ cup pasta water.

Steam broccoli 5 minutes, or until tender. Sauté garlic in 1 tablespoon heated oil in skillet for 1 minute, or until golden brown.

In a bowl, combine pasta, reserved pasta water, broccoli, garlic, remaining oil, and cheese. Toss well. Season with salt and pepper to taste and toss again. Serves 8.

Mexican Macaroni and Cheese

1 (8-ounce) package large elbow macaroni
1 (8-ounce) box Mexican Velveeta cheese, cubed small
1 teaspoon taco seasoning
½ cup salsa
¼ cup thinly sliced green onions

Cook macaroni according to package directions; drain. Combine macaroni with cheese and taco seasoning. Stir in salsa, then sprinkle with green onions. Pour into a greased 2-quart casserole dish. Bake in 350° oven for 20 minutes, or till hot and bubbly.

Superb Baked Mac and Cheese

1 (8-ounce) package elbow macaroni
½ stick butter, melted
¼ cup flour
2 cups milk
2 cups shredded sharp Cheddar cheese, divided

Cook macaroni in boiling salted water 7 minutes. Drain well, then spoon into buttered casserole. Stir together butter and flour until smooth, then add milk and cheese; mix well. Add to macaroni and stir well to combine. Bake at 350° about 20 minutes.

Baked Pimento and Cheese

2 slices bread, torn into pieces
½ cup milk
1 (1-pound) block sharp Cheddar cheese, grated
1 egg, beaten
1 (2-ounce) bottle diced pimentos

Soak bread in milk. Combine with cheese, egg, and pimentos. Pour into greased 2-quart casserole, and bake at 350° for 25–30 minutes.

Shrimp Scampi Pasta in a Flash

1 (8-ounce) package spaghetti
1 stick butter
1½ cups dry white wine
2 pounds shrimp, peeled, deveined
1 teaspoon dried basil

Bring a large pot of salted water to a boil. Add pasta and cook 8–10 minutes; drain. In a large saucepan or skillet over medium heat, melt butter, then add white wine, shrimp, and basil. Cook until shrimp are pink, 3–5 minutes. Serve over pasta. Serves 6–8.

Ham and Pasta Toss

1 (12-ounce) package pasta (any type)
2 tablespoons olive oil
1 (14-ounce) can chicken broth
¾ teaspoon dried basil, crumbled (or 1 tablespoon fresh)
4 ounces boiled ham, thinly sliced, cut into ½-inch strips

Cook pasta according to package directions. Heat oil in medium saucepan over medium heat. Pour in broth; add basil and cook 3 minutes, or until it begins to boil. Pour pasta into large colander to drain. Return pasta to pan and combine with broth mixture. Add ham and toss well. Cook about 2 minutes over medium-high heat; serve piping hot. May sprinkle with Parmesan cheese, if desired. Serves 4.

Tangy Tequila Chicken Fettuccini

1 (8-ounce) package fettuccini
1 (15-ounce) jar Alfredo sauce
¼ cup tequila
1 teaspoon lime zest
2 (6-ounce) packages grilled chicken breast strips

Cook fettuccini in boiling salted water; drain. Just before pasta is done, cook Alfredo sauce, tequila, and lime zest in a saucepan just to boiling. Remove from heat. Add chicken strips, and heat through. In a large serving bowl, toss hot fettuccini with tequila sauce. Serves 6.

Editor's Extra: To add color, sprinkle with diced red bell pepper.

The workweek, in most of the industrialized world, is **five** working days.

The legal workweek varies from nation to nation, and its definition is usually heavily influenced by the predominant religion of the country, or by colonial history. Most countries in Europe, the Americas, and East Asia have a business week defined as Monday through Friday.

The legal workweek in the Muslim world is either Saturday through Wednesday (as in Saudi Arabia), or Sunday through Thursday (as in Egypt and Israel).

Muenster Chicken Bake

2 cups ziti pasta, cooked, drained
1 (12-ounce) can chicken, drained
2 cups shredded Muenster cheese
1 (10¾-ounce) can cream of chicken soup
¼ cup grated Parmesan cheese

Preheat oven to 350°. Combine pasta, chicken, Muenster cheese, soup, and 1 soup can water, and pour into a greased 2-quart casserole dish. Sprinkle with Parmesan cheese. Bake 30–35 minutes or until hot and bubbly. Serves 6.

Quick and Delicious Lasagna

1½ (26-ounce) jars spaghetti sauce, divided
1 (8-ounce) package lasagna noodles (9 strips)
1 pound ricotta or cottage cheese
1 (8-ounce) package shredded mozzarella cheese
1 cup grated Parmesan cheese

Spread about 1 cup sauce in a greased 9x13x2-inch baking pan. On top of sauce, arrange a layer of half the uncooked lasagna. Top with ⅓ of the remaining sauce, ½ the ricotta, ⅓ the mozzarella, and ⅓ the Parmesan. Repeat, gently pressing remaining lasagna pieces into cheese mixture below. Pour remaining sauce over, making sure all lasagna pieces are covered with sauce. Top with remaining mozzarella and Parmesan. Cover with foil, and bake at 350° for 30 minutes. Uncover and bake another 20 minutes, until lightly browned and bubbling. Wait at least 10 minutes before cutting and serving. Serves 8.

Ravioli Rockefeller

1 (29-ounce) jar spaghetti sauce, divided
1 (16-ounce) package frozen cheese ravioli
1 (10-ounce) package frozen chopped spinach,
thawed, drained well (squeeze)
1 pound ground beef or Italian sausage, browned,
drained
1 (8-ounce) package shredded mozzarella cheese

Spoon ½ cup spaghetti sauce in bottom of a greased 2-quart casserole. Place frozen ravioli on top of sauce. Top ravioli with spinach. Top spinach with ground beef or Italian sausage. Top meat with remaining spaghetti sauce. Top sauce with mozzarella cheese. Cover tightly with foil and bake at 350° for 45 minutes. Remove foil and continue baking for 10 minutes, until cheese is bubbly.

S'ghetti Bake

1 pound ground beef
1 (8-ounce) package mostaccioli pasta, cooked
1 (26-ounce) jar spaghetti sauce
½ cup grated Parmesan cheese
1 (8-ounce) package shredded mozzarella cheese

Brown ground beef in large skillet; drain. Stir in pasta, spaghetti sauce, and Parmesan cheese. Pour into a 9x13-inch casserole. Top with mozzarella. Bake at 375° for 20 minutes. Serves 8.

A military aircraft pilot who has destroyed **five** or more enemy aircraft in air-to-air combat is known as an ace. In all the years of air combat from World War I to the present, over 5,400 pilots have become aces.

Erich Hartmann of Germany is the all-time leader with 352 enemy aircraft shot down in World War II.

Manfred von Richthofen (better known as the Red Baron), also a German, is still regarded today as the "ace of aces." He was an air squadron leader and flying ace, and the most successful fighter pilot of World War I, credited with 80 confirmed air combat victories.

In the comic strip *Peanuts*, one of Snoopy's fantasies portrays him as a World War I flying ace with a personal grudge against the Red Baron.

Good Ole Throw-Together

1½ pounds ground beef
1½ teaspoons Creole seasoning
1 (16-ounce) can pinto beans
1 (14½-ounce) can petit diced tomatoes
1 (8-ounce) package elbow macaroni or bow tie pasta,
  or mixture

Brown ground beef with seasoning in large skillet; drain. Add undrained beans, undrained tomatoes, and pasta. Cover and cook on medium-high heat until bubbling. Reduce heat, and simmer 20–25 minutes. Check liquid, adding water if needed. Top with Parmesan cheese, if desired.

Pork Steak with Noodles

1 pound pork steak, cut in 1-inch cubes
1 (14½-ounce) can diced tomatoes
1½ cups chopped celery
1 onion, chopped
1 (16-ounce) package medium egg noodles

In nonstick skillet, fry pork until brown; drain. Add tomatoes, celery, and onion; simmer covered ½ hour. Cook noodles; drain.

  Preheat oven to 300°. Pour meat mixture over noodles and stir. Bake in greased casserole 1 hour.

A Very Fine Pilaf

½ cup broken (1-inch) angel hair pasta
3 tablespoons butter or margarine
1 (14-ounce) can beef or chicken broth
⅓ cup water
½ cup raw long-grain rice

In saucepan, brown noodles in butter, stirring till browned. Add remaining ingredients. Season to taste. Bring to a boil; reduce heat. Cover and simmer 20–25 minutes, until liquid is absorbed. Serves 4–5.

Southern Red Rice

2 cups rice
¼ cup bacon drippings
1 (14½-ounce) can diced tomatoes
1 teaspoon salt
1 quart chicken broth

Sauté rice in bacon drippings over medium-high heat for 1 minute, stirring constantly. Add tomatoes, salt, and chicken broth, and bring to a boil. Lower heat to medium-low, and simmer covered about 20 minutes, until rice is tender.

Really 'Rific Rice

This recipe can be doubled or tripled. Goes great with anything.

1 cup uncooked long-grain rice
1 (10-ounce) can beef consommé
1 (10¾-ounce) can French onion soup
1 (4-ounce) can mushrooms, drained
½ stick butter

Mix all ingredients in casserole dish. Bake in a 350° oven, uncovered, for about an hour, stirring every 15 minutes or until all juice is absorbed. If it gets dry, add a little butter or water. Serves 6.

Pecan Wild Rice Supreme

3 tablespoons butter
⅓ cup chopped green onions
⅓ cup raisins
⅓ cup chopped pecans
2 cups cooked wild rice

Melt butter over medium-high heat. Sauté green onions, raisins, and pecans till onions are tender. Remove from heat, and stir in rice. Toss, and serve warm.

Spicy Sausage Jambalaya

1 (1-pound) package smoked sausage, sliced
2 (10-ounce) cans mild Ro-Tel tomatoes
2 (14-ounce) cans chicken broth
1½ teaspoons Creole seasoning
1½ cups uncooked long-grain rice

Brown sausage in large skillet. Stir in tomatoes, broth, and seasoning; bring to a boil. Add rice, cover, and simmer 25 minutes. Uncover and cook until liquid is absorbed. Serves 6–8.

Editor's Extra: Brown ⅓ cup chopped onion and/or bell pepper with sausage for a more authentic Cajun jambalaya taste.

Black Beans, Chicken, and Rice

2 (7-ounce) boxes Spanish rice
2 (6-ounce) packages cooked chicken strips, chopped
5 slices bacon, cooked, crumbled
1½ cups shredded mozzarella cheese
1 (15-ounce) can black beans, rinsed, drained

Prepare rice according to package instructions. Mix remaining ingredients in a large bowl and set aside. When rice is just cooked, mix chicken mixture into rice, cover, and let stand about 10 minutes. Serve topped with chopped tomato and green onions. Serves 6–8.

Mexi-Broccoli Rice Casserole

2 (10-ounce) packages frozen broccoli, thawed, drained
1 (15-ounce) can Mexican-style whole-kernel corn
2 cups cooked white rice
1 (10¾-ounce) can cream of mushroom soup
1 (15-ounce) jar Mexican Cheez Whiz

Mix all ingredients in a large bowl, then pour into a greased 9x13-inch baking dish. Bake at 350° for 30 minutes, until lightly brown on top.

Red Bean Rally

1 (8-ounce) package dried kidney beans
1 cup raw rice, cooked
10–12 pieces thick-sliced bacon or salt pork, chopped
1 cup frozen seasoning blend
1–3 garlic cloves, minced

Put beans in large pot, and cover with water. Cook, covered, at a slow boil 3–4 hours, adding water as needed (juice should be thick).

Fry bacon, reserving drippings; add to beans. Sauté onion and garlic in drippings; add to beans along with salt to taste. Serve beans, bacon, and juice over hot rice. Serves 8.

Editor's Extra: If you can't find frozen seasoning blend in the frozen vegetable section of your grocery store, you can make up your own mix of chopped onions, bell peppers, celery, and parsley.

The **five** stages of grief, as defined by Swiss-born psychiatrist Elisabeth Kübler-Ross in her book *On Death and Dying* (1969), are denial, anger, bargaining, depression, and acceptance.

Curried Ramen and Rice

1 envelope boil-in-a-bag brown rice
1 package ramen noodles
1 tablespoon curry powder
1 cup chopped Chinese parsley
½ cup raisins

Boil rice in boiling water; drain pot and empty rice packet back into pot; cover to keep warm. Break up ramen noodles while still in package with hands. Open package, remove spice package, and mix crushed noodles with cooked brown rice. The heat of the rice cooks the noodles. Add spice packet, curry powder, parsley, and raisins. Great hot or cold. Serves 4–6.

Two Pizzas in a Skillet

1 loaf round bread
5 tablespoons olive oil, divided
4–6 tablespoons Italian seasoning (or herbs of choice)
2 (8-ounce) cans tomato sauce
4 cups shredded cheese blend

Cut bread in half, making 2 round loaves. Heat half the oil in a frying pan until it just begins to smoke. Sprinkle in herbs. Add 1 can tomato sauce; stir as it begins to bubble. Sprinkle half the cheese evenly over sauce. Lay 1 round loaf cut-side-down in sauce. Let it simmer about 30 seconds. Turn it upside down onto a plate and cut into wedges to serve. Repeat with other half of bread loaf.

Editor's Extra: Mushrooms, pepperoni, etc. may be added to skillet, if desired.

Fast
and
Fabulous

FIVE ★ STAR

Meats

Meatball Quesadillas

½ cup chopped onion
2 tablespoons olive oil, divided
4 large flour tortillas
1 package frozen precooked meatballs, any flavor, thawed, sliced
1 (8-ounce) bag shredded double pizza or quesadilla cheese

Sauté onion in a tablespoon of olive oil to soften. Drain and set aside. Preheat oven to 375°. Spread a teaspoon of oil with the back of a spoon or a pastry brush on one side of flour tortilla. Place tortilla, oiled side down, on cookie sheet. Layer sliced meatballs, onions, and cheese on top. Top with a second tortilla; press together slightly and brush top with olive oil. Repeat process with remaining ingredients. Bake 10–15 minutes, or until tortillas are brown and crisp. Cut into wedges to serve.

Sweet and Sour Swedish Meatballs

¾ cup apple jelly
⅓ cup spicy brown mustard
⅓ cup whiskey or apple juice
1½ teaspoons Worcestershire
1 (38-ounce) bag frozen Swedish meatballs, thawed

In a large saucepan, combine all ingredients except meatballs. Heat to boiling, and add meatballs, gently stirring until well coated. Cook over medium heat until heated through.

Red Top Meatloaf

Good enough for company . . . easy enough for every day.

1½ pounds ground chuck
1 egg
1 tablespoon onion flakes
½ cup cracker crumbs
½ cup chili sauce, divided

Preheat oven to 350°. Mix ground meat, egg, onion flakes, cracker crumbs, and ⅓ cup chili sauce with hands. Shape into loaf; place in 9x5-inch loaf pan. Cover with remaining chili sauce. Bake 55–60 minutes. Serves 6.

A Small Meatloaf

This is quick to cook and ideal for serving two or three people.

¾ pound ground beef
7 crackers, crumbled
½ cup frozen seasoning blend
2 tablespoons Worcestershire
⅓ cup ketchup, divided

Preheat oven to 375°. Mix first 4 ingredients, plus salt and pepper to taste, and ½ the ketchup. Flatten in small casserole dish. Bake 20 minutes. Remove and drain grease. Coat top with remaining ketchup. Bake another 10 minutes. Slice and serve.

Editor's Extra: If you can't find frozen seasoning blend in the frozen vegetable section of your grocery store, you can make up your own mix of chopped onions, bell peppers, celery, and parsley.

Located on the Inner Harbor of Baltimore, Maryland, the Baltimore World Trade Center is the world's tallest equilateral **five**-sided building. With an elevation of 423 feet and 27 stories, the building features a 360-degree panoramic view of Baltimore.

The **five**-sided JP Morgan Chase Tower in Houston, Texas, is taller, but has unequal sides. The Sky Lobby is 60 stories above the plaza level. The view from this lobby is enhanced through the use of wide glass spans and thirteen-foot ceilings. A fascinating aspect of the Tower is its "**fifth side**," designed to be free of columns to enjoy an uninterrupted twenty-mile vista of Houston.

Simply Delicious Goulash

This old-fashioned recipe is simply delicious.

3 cups elbow macaroni
1 pound ground chuck
1 (12-ounce) bag frozen seasoning blend
1 (10¾-ounce) can tomato soup
2 (14½-ounce) cans diced tomatoes with garlic

Cook pasta according to package directions; drain and set aside. Meanwhile, cook meat and seasoning blend in 10-inch skillet until meat is browned, stirring to break up meat. Drain well. Add soup and diced tomatoes, and heat through, stirring frequently. Stir in pasta, then pour into a greased 3-quart casserole. Bake at 350° about 50 minutes, until bubbly and hot. Serves 6.

Editor's Extra: If you can't find frozen seasoning blend in the frozen vegetable section of your grocery store, you can make up your own mix of chopped onions, bell peppers, celery, and parsley.

Best-Ever Tamale Bake

2 (15-ounce) cans tamales, paper removed
½ cup chopped onion
2 (16-ounce) cans chili without beans
1 cup shredded Cheddar cheese
1½ cups crushed Fritos

Preheat oven to 350°. Grease a 9x13-inch baking dish. Cut tamales into bite-size pieces, and place in prepared baking dish. Sprinkle tamales with onion, then spread with chili. Bake covered for 45 minutes. Add cheese immediately after removing from oven. Once cheese melts, sprinkle with crushed Fritos.

Barbecue Stuffed Potatoes

4 large baking potatoes
1 (18-ounce) container barbecue pulled beef or pork
1 stick butter or margarine, divided
1 cup shredded Cheddar cheese
⅓ cup chopped green onions

Bake potatoes in oven at 400° for 1 hour till punchy soft. Meanwhile, heat barbecue meat on low. Cut baked potatoes in half lengthwise, and add ⅛ stick butter to each half, fluffing pulp and butter with a spoon to mix. Put each half on a serving plate and pile warm barbecue meat on top, adding a generous sprinkling of cheese and some green onions to each. Serves 8 (or maybe just 4 hungry men).

Potato Tacos

1 pound ground chuck
1 envelope taco seasoning
4 russet potatoes, baked
1 cup shredded sharp Cheddar cheese
1 cup chopped green onions

Brown beef; drain. Add taco seasoning with water according to package directions. While still hot, cut an X in the top of each potato; fluff with a fork. Top with taco meat, cheese, and onions. Serve with salsa and sour cream, if desired. Serves 4.

Mexi Meal in a Pan

2 pounds ground chuck, browned
1 (10-ounce) can Ro-Tel tomatoes, or 1 (16-ounce) jar
medium-hot salsa
1 envelope taco seasoning
2 (8-count) cans refrigerated crescent rolls
1 (8-ounce) box Mexican Velveeta, sliced

Preheat oven to 400°. Combine browned ground chuck with Ro-Tel tomatoes and taco seasoning; set aside. Form a crust by pressing 1 can crescent rolls into bottom of a lightly greased 9x13-inch baking pan. Layer beef mixture and cheese on top of crust. Arrange remaining can of crescent rolls on top. Bake 15–20 minutes. Serves 8.

Editor's Extra: Serve with salsa, shredded lettuce, chopped tomatoes, sliced black olives, or sour cream, if desired.

Chili Corn Chip Pie

2 tablespoons butter
4–5 cups crushed corn chips or tostadas, divided
2 small onions, chopped
2 (16-ounce) cans chili without beans
3 cups (mixed) grated Monterey Jack and Cheddar

Melt butter in 3-quart casserole dish; cover bottom with ½ of crushed chips. Place onions on top of chips, then chili. Top with remaining chips. Sprinkle top generously with cheese. Bake in 350° oven 15 minutes.

Farmer's Pie

1½ pounds ground beef
1 cup frozen seasoning blend
2 (15-ounce) cans Italian green beans, drained
2–3 cups leftover mashed potatoes
¾ cup shredded Colby-Jack cheese

Brown meat and seasoning in large skillet until tender; drain. Place meat mixture in bottom of 3-quart casserole dish. Top with green beans; season with black pepper to taste, if desired. Spread layer of mashed potatoes over green beans and top with shredded cheese. Bake in 350° oven 25–30 minutes.

Editor's Extra: If you can't find frozen seasoning blend in the frozen vegetable section of your grocery store, you can make up your own mix of chopped onions, bell peppers, celery, and parsley.

One-Pot Hamburger and Fries

2 pounds ground chuck
1 onion, chopped
1 (10¾-ounce) can cream of mushroom soup
1 (10¾-ounce) can Cheddar cheese soup
1 (20-ounce) package frozen crinkle-cut fries, thawed

Brown meat with onions in large oven-proof skillet over medium-high heat; drain, if necessary. Stir in soups. Top with fries. Bake uncovered in 350° oven for 40 minutes, or till fries are golden brown.

The **five** most populated countries in the world (late 2006) are:

- China–1,314,198,715
- India–1,121,190,850
- United States–300,278,015
- Indonesia–245,452,740
- Brazil–188,650,227

(The 2006 world population is approximately 6,560,000,000.)

The **five** largest countries in terms of area (square miles) are:

- Russia–6,591,027
- Canada–3,854,082
- United States–3,717,727
- China–3,704,426
- Brazil–3,285,618

Grilled Tex-Mex Cheeseburger

1 pound ground beef
1 envelope ranch dressing mix
¼ cup taco sauce
1 egg, beaten
⅓ cup shredded Cheddar cheese

Combine meat, ranch dressing mix, taco sauce, egg, and cheese. Mix well, and shape into 4 patties; grill till done. Serve on toasted buns with trimmings of your choice.

Surprise Cheeseburgers

1½ pounds ground beef
Worcestershire to taste
4 tomato slices
4 onion slices
4 slices Cheddar cheese

Sprinkle meat generously with Worcestershire, and shape into 8 thin patties. On half the patties, place 1 slice tomato, onion, and 1 slice cheese. Cover with remaining patties. Seal patties together, and sprinkle with salt and pepper to taste. Grill 10–12 minutes on each side. Serve on toasted buns or as an entrée with a salad and hash browns. Serves 4.

Brian's Favorite Sloppy Joes

1½ pounds ground round
8 tablespoons tomato paste
1 tablespoon sugar
1 (12-ounce) jar salsa
8 hamburger buns

In a large skillet over medium-high heat, cook meat until browned, breaking up the meat while cooking. Add remaining ingredients; mix well. Season to taste. Reduce heat to a simmer, and cook partially covered, 45 minutes, stirring occasionally. Serve in hamburger buns. Serves 8.

Frankfurter Burgers

1 pound ground sirloin
½ cup barbecue sauce
4 tablespoons pickle relish
2 tablespoons minced onion
Hot dog buns

Combine meat, barbecue sauce, relish, and onion, and shape into hot dog-shaped patties. Brown in skillet, turning frequently to cook evenly, till done (about 5 minutes). Place in hot dog buns with condiments of your choice.

Pizza-licious Casserole

1 pound ground chuck
1 (15-ounce) can chunky Italian-style tomato sauce
1 (4-ounce) can sliced mushrooms, drained
1 (10-ounce) can refrigerated pizza crust dough
1 (8-ounce) package shredded mozzarella cheese,
  divided

Brown meat in 10-inch skillet on medium-high heat. Drain, if necessary. Add tomato sauce and mushrooms, and heat through.

Spray a 9x13-inch baking dish with nonstick spray. Press pizza crust into bottom and halfway up sides of dish. Spread half of mozzarella cheese on bottom of crust, then top with meat mixture. Bake uncovered at 425° for 12 minutes. Top with remaining cheese. Bake an additional 5 minutes, or until crust is browned and cheese is melted. Serves 6.

Pizza Muffin Cups

1 (8-count) can flaky Grands biscuits
1 (10-ounce) jar pizza sauce
1 pound ground beef, cooked (or meat of choice)
1 (4-ounce) can sliced mushrooms, drained
Shredded mozzarella cheese

Preheat oven to 350°. Halve biscuit layers horizontally, and press into 16 greased muffin cups. Add a spoonful of pizza sauce into each. Add some meat and mushrooms. Top with cheese. Bake at 350° for 15–20 minutes.

Crocked Cajun Roast

1 (2-pound) boneless beef chuck roast
1 tablespoon Cajun seasoning
1 large onion, chopped
1 (14½-ounce) can diced tomatoes with garlic
½ teaspoon Tabasco

Sprinkle roast with Cajun seasoning, and rub in well. Place in crockpot and sprinkle with onion. Pour tomatoes over roast, and sprinkle with Tabasco. Cover and cook on LOW setting 8–10 hours. Serves 6.

Sunday Best Aroma Roast

This fills your house with such a magnificent aroma, you simply can't wait for it to be done. Watch out for early tasters . . . they can't stop with just one bite!

3 cloves garlic
1 (3- to 4-pound) rump roast
1 tablespoon olive oil
1 teaspoon Cajun seasoning
6 pats butter

Slice garlic, then slice again into small sticks. Stab holes all over roast, inserting a garlic stick into each hole. Cover and refrigerate overnight, or at least a few hours.

While oven is preheating to 350°, place roast in roaster pan, and rub with olive oil, then sprinkle all over with seasoning. Put some butter pats under roast and some on top. Roast 2½–3 hours till nicely browned. Serves 6–8.

Editor's Extra: Sometimes you get a cut of meat that is just not as tender as others, so if it doesn't slice tenderly, cover and cook it for another 40 minutes or so. I like to put baking potatoes in alongside during the last hour of roasting, and serve au jus over all.

The five top-selling books of all time are:

1. *The Holy Bible* – 6 billion
2. *Quotations from Chariman Mao Tse Tung* – 900 million
3. *The American Spelling Book by Noah Webster* – 100 million
4. *Guiness World Records* – 94 million
5. *The World Alamanac Book of Facts* – 73.5 million

One of the big screen's most enduring franchises launched in 1934. *The Thin Man,* starring William Powell and Myrna Loy, would eventually spawn **five** sequels:

- *After the Thin Man*
- *Another Thin Man*
- *Shadow of the Thin Man*
- *The Thin Man Goes Home*
- *Song of the Thin Man*

Other movies that had **five** sequels:

A Nightmare on Elm Street (1984)

- *Freddy's Revenge*
- *Dream Warriors*
- *The Dream Master*
- *The Dream Child*
- *Freddy's Dead: The Final Nightmare*

Leprechaun (1993)

- *Leprechaun 2*
- *Leprechaun 3*
- *Leprechaun 4: In Space*
- *Leprechaun in the Hood*
- *Leprechaun: Back 2 the Hood*

Lumpless Aroma Roast Gravy

Once you serve this, don't be surprised if you're asked to make the gravy every time!

1 cup au jus from roast
1¼ cups hot tap water
2½ tablespoons flour
1 teaspoon beef bouillon granules
½ teaspoon browning sauce

Heat au jus. In a pint jar, shake hot water and flour till smooth, then pour slowly while stirring into hot au jus. Lower heat and add bouillon, browning sauce, and salt and pepper to taste. Add more shaken warm flour-water or just hot water to thicken or thin. Superb over rice.

Editor's Extra: If you have more or less than a cup of au jus, simply adjust flour and water.

Drunken Crockpot Roast

Makes a delicious au jus.

1 (5- to 6-pound) chuck roast
2 (10¾-ounce) cans French onion soup
1½ (12-ounce) cans beer
1 teaspoon coarsely ground black pepper
2 beef bouillon cubes

Cook roast in 400° oven for one hour. Move roast to large crockpot. Add remaining ingredients. Stir, and cook on HIGH 4–5 hours, or till tender. Or cook on LOW overnight.

Roast Beef Hash

2–3 tablespoons butter
1 onion, finely chopped
1 cup chopped, cooked roast
2 cups beef broth (or leftover au jus from roast)
1 large potato, peeled, cubed

Melt butter in a 10-inch skillet. Cook onion and roast till onion is soft. Add boiling beef broth (or au jus) and potato. Lower heat, cover skillet, and allow ingredients to cook slowly until tender. Serve over rice, toast, or biscuits. Serves 3–4.

Corned Beef Hash

⅓ cup oil
1 (24-ounce) package frozen O'Brien potatoes
1 (12-ounce) can corned beef, cubed
½ teaspoon salt
¼ teaspoon pepper

Heat oil in large nonstick skillet over medium-high heat. Add O'Brien potatoes and cook, turning occasionally, until nicely browned. Add corned beef, mix well, and allow to brown with potatoes, about 5 minutes, turning frequently. Season with salt and pepper.

Cabbage and Corned Beef

1 head cabbage, chopped
1 large onion, minced
1 (12-ounce) can corned beef, chopped
½ teaspoon black pepper
1 tablespoon red pepper flakes (or more)

Cook cabbage and onion on low heat in a little olive oil, stirring frequently, until cabbage is cooked down and wilted. Add corned beef, and mix well. Stir in black pepper and red pepper flakes. Cover and simmer about 25 minutes, stirring occasionally.

Coca-Cola Brisket

1 envelope onion soup mix
1 (12-ounce) can Coca Cola (not diet)
1 (10-ounce) bottle A-1 steak sauce
1 teaspoon black pepper
1 (6-pound) brisket, trimmed

Preheat oven to 325°. Combine onion soup mix, Coca Cola, steak sauce, and pepper. Place brisket (fat side up) in large roasting pan, and pour sauce over. Bake, covered, at 325° for 5 hours or till tender.

Fast Steaks au Poivre

And we do mean fast! Do this when you are ready to serve.

2 teaspoons cracked black pepper
4 (1-inch) tenderloin, Delmonico, or strip steaks
1 tablespoon olive oil
2–3 tablespoons brandy
1 tablespoon butter

Pepper steaks heavily, pressing into steaks. Heat a large skillet till hot, then add oil. Brown steaks on medium-high heat, then turn to brown other side to desired doneness. Remove steaks to plates. Deglaze pan with brandy (or lemon juice and Worcestershire), and pour over each steak. Melt butter in pan, and pour this over each steak. Superb!

Perfectly Cooked Melt-In-Your-Mouth Rib-Eyes

These steaks are crusty on one side, soft on the other, and perfect in the middle.

3 tablespoons vegetable oil
4 rib-eye steaks
1 teaspoon salt, or to taste
1 teaspoon black pepper, or to taste
2 tablespoons butter

Preheat oven to 450°. Heat oil in oven-proof skillet. Sear seasoned steaks well only on one side, about 2 minutes. Carefully transfer skillet to hot oven—do not turn steaks. Cook about 12 minutes, more or less, to your desired doneness. Put on plate crusty side up, and add a pat of butter to top of each steak. Offer steak sauce, but it's great without it!

Teriyaki Steak

1 (2½-pound) chuck steak (about 1½ inches thick)
1½ teaspoons meat tenderizer
⅔ cup teriyaki sauce
1 (6-ounce) can tomato paste
¼ cup oil

Sprinkle meat with meat tenderizer according to label directions. Combine teriyaki sauce, tomato paste, and oil; brush over meat. Place on grill 3–4 inches from hot coals. Cook about 15 minutes. Turn steak over and brush with additional sauce. Cook to desired degree of doneness. Heat remaining sauce and serve with steak. Serves 4.

Slaughterhouse Five is a 1969 novel by best-selling author Kurt Vonnegut. It is one of his most popular works and widely regarded as a classic. Vonnegut combines science fiction elements with an analysis of the human condition from an uncommon perspective, using time travel as a plot device.

"**Slaughterhouse-Five**" refers to the slaughterhouse in which the main character, Billy Pilgrim, stays as a POW in Dresden during the firebombing. (This parallels Vonnegut's own experience as a prisoner of war in Dresden.)

Slaughterhouse-Five was listed by *Time Magazine* as one of the hundred best English-language books from 1923 to present.

A successful film adaptation of the book, also called *Slaughterhouse-Five*, was made in 1972.

Oven-Baked Chuck Steak

1½ pounds boneless chuck steak
2 envelopes dry onion soup mix
1 tablespoon Worcestershire
¼ teaspoon black pepper
1 (2½-ounce) jar sliced mushrooms, drained

Preheat oven to 375°. Line shallow baking dish with foil. Add roast, and sprinkle both sides with onion soup mix, Worcestershire, and pepper. Top with mushrooms. Wrap loosely with foil, sealing completely with a double fold. Bake about 1 hour, or until tender. Serves 4.

Round Steak and Mushroom Bake

2 pounds round steak (not thin sliced)
1 (4½-ounce) jar sliced mushrooms, drained
½ cup frozen seasoning blend
1 envelope dry onion soup mix
1½ teaspoons beef bouillon granules

Cut round steak into serving pieces and put into large shallow pan. Put mushrooms on top of meat. Add seasoning blend. Sprinkle top with onion soup mix and beef bouillon. Add 2 packages of water (using onion soup envelope). Wrap tightly with foil. Bake at 350° for 2 hours. Serve with rice.

Editor's Extra: If you can't find frozen seasoning blend in the frozen vegetable section of your grocery store, you can make up your own mix of chopped onions, bell peppers, celery, and parsley.

5

Fried Round Steak

1½ pounds top round steak (½ inch thick)
1 egg, beaten
1 tablespoon milk
1 cup finely crushed crackers
¼ cup cooking oil

Pound steak ¼ inch thick, then cut into bite-size pieces. Beat egg with milk. Dip steak in egg mixture, then coat with crumbs. Brown steak in hot oil over medium heat, turning once. Cover, and cook over medium-low heat 45–60 minutes or until tender. Season with salt and pepper.

Tangy Brown Barbecue Sauce

¼ cup prepared mustard
2 tablespoons molasses
2 teaspoons Tabasco
2 tablespoons vinegar
2 tablespoons Worcestershire

Combine mustard, molasses, Tabasco, vinegar, and Worcestershire; blend well. Brush on your favorite meat during cooking.

Pepper Jelly Ribs

1 (12-ounce) can beer
1 (8-ounce) can crushed pineapple, undrained
1 (8-ounce) jar pepper jelly
1 (18-ounce) bottle barbecue sauce
2 pounds beef short ribs

Combine beer, pineapple and juice, and pepper jelly in medium bowl. Marinate ribs in this several hours, or overnight.

Remove ribs, and reserve marinade. Grill ribs over low heat 1½–2 hours, basting occasionally with barbecue sauce and reserved marinade.

Best Baby Backs Evah!

4–5 pounds baby back ribs (2 racks)
⅓ cup Italian salad dressing
1½ (18-ounce) bottles barbecue sauce
1 (26-ounce) jar spaghetti sauce
1¼ cups brown sugar

Using heavy-duty foil, line a big roasting pan, and lay ribs on foil. Pour dressing and sauces over ribs, then sugar over all. (Use 2 pans if necessary; just be sure ribs are mostly covered with sauce.) Bake uncovered at 250° about 6 hours.

Editor's Extra: You can use any brand or flavor of sauces, and that gives you many variations in flavor. And that's a good thing, because you'll never want to cook ribs any other way.

Crockpot Coca-Cola Ribs

3 pounds boneless country-style ribs
½ teaspoon garlic salt
½ teaspoon crushed red pepper
½ cup Coca-Cola
⅔ cup barbecue sauce

Cut ribs into serving-size portions and place in crockpot. Season with garlic salt and pepper. Add Coca-Cola. Cover and cook on LOW about 8 hours, or until tender. During last 30 minutes of cook time, drain juice from ribs, then coat well with barbecue sauce.

Country-Style Cajun Ribs

3 pounds country-style ribs
1 tablespoon Cajun seasoning
1 tablespoon chili powder
1¼ teaspoons onion salt
¼ teaspoon cumin

Cook ribs in water to cover for 1 hour and 15 minutes. Remove from water, and season with Cajun seasoning, chili powder, onion salt, and cumin; rub into ribs. Grill over medium heat or bake in 350° oven 35–45 minutes, or until done.

Cran-Cherry-Sauced Pork Tenderloin

1 (1-pound) pork tenderloin
¾ cup cranberry juice
2 teaspoons spicy brown mustard
1 teaspoon cornstarch
1 (16-ounce) can dark pitted sweet cherries, drained

Cut tenderloin crosswise into 1-inch thick medallions. Flatten each medallion with palm of your hand, pressing into ½-inch thickness.

Spray a large skillet with nonstick cooking spray, and heat over medium-high heat. Sear pork 6 minutes, until meat is slightly pink in center, turning once. Remove from skillet; cover and keep warm.

In same skillet, combine remaining ingredients except cherries. Cook over medium heat until thickened and bubbly, stirring constantly. Remove from heat, stir in cherries, and serve over pork medallions.

The top **five** wealthiest people in the world (2006):

1. William Gates
   United States
   Software (Microsoft)
2. Warren Buffett
   United States
   Investments
   (Berkshire Hathaway)
3. Carlos Slim Helú
   Mexico
   Telecommunications
   (MCI, among others)
4. Ingvar Kamprad
   Sweden
   Retailing (IKEA)
5. Lakshmi Mittal
   India
   Steel manufacturing
   (Mittal Steel)

Melinda's Crockpot Tequila Pork

1 (4-pound) pork tenderloin roast
¼ cup tequila
1 lime, juiced
2 teaspoons seasoning salt
1 (4-ounce) can diced green chiles, drained

Place pork roast in crockpot. Pour tequila and lime juice over roast. Sprinkle with seasoning salt. Sprinkle green chiles evenly over all. Cook on LOW 6–8 hours.

Editor's Extra: This is superb shredded in its juice, and wrapped in warm flour tortillas. To make it even more special, offer the usual Mexican garnishes: lettuce, tomatoes, cheese, guacamole, etc.

Sweet Apple Glazed Pork Roast

1 (4- to 6-pound) pork loin roast
⅓ cup applesauce
¼ cup molasses
¼ teaspoon ground ginger
1 clove garlic, minced

Place roast on rack, fat side up, in roasting pan. Insert meat thermometer into thickest part of roast, making sure not to touch bone. Bake at 325° for about 2 hours, or until meat thermometer registers 170°.

Combine applesauce, molasses, ginger, and garlic in saucepan over medium heat. Baste with applesauce mixture every 10 minutes during last 30 minutes of cooking. Serve pork with remaining applesauce mixture. Serves 8.

Fabulous Rosemary Pork Chops

2 teaspoons crushed dried rosemary
¼ cup brown sugar
¾ cup water
1½ cups soy sauce
4 thick pork chops

In medium bowl with lid, combine rosemary, brown sugar, water, and soy sauce. Add pork chops, and marinate in refrigerator, covered, 4 hours. Transfer all to casserole dish and bake in 350° oven, uncovered, 40–60 minutes, or until done.

Pork Chops and Gravy

4 (½-inch-thick) bone-in pork chops
½ cup all-purpose flour, divided
½ cup oil
½ cup evaporated milk
½ cup water

Coat pork chops with ¼ cup flour. Heat oil in large, heavy skillet over medium-high heat. Fry chops in hot oil on both sides till golden brown, about 10 minutes; season with salt and pepper to taste while frying. Remove chops and set aside, reserving drippings.

Combine evaporated milk and water; set aside. Heat pan drippings over medium-high heat till hot, then add remaining ¼ cup flour; cook, stirring constantly, about a minute. Add milk-water mixture, and stir quickly to blend. Bring to a boil, and boil 1 minute, then lower heat and simmer about 5 minutes. Season with salt and pepper to taste. Add pork chops to gravy, and simmer over medium-low heat till very tender, about 30 minutes.

Souper Scrumptious Pork Chops

6 pork chops
1 (4-ounce) can sliced mushrooms, drained
1 package dry onion soup mix
1 (10¾-ounce) can cream of mushroom soup
¼ soup can milk

In large skillet, brown pork chops on both sides, then place in a lightly greased 9x13-inch baking dish. Season with salt and pepper to taste. Sprinkle mushrooms over top. Combine soup mix, cream of mushroom soup, and milk, and pour over all. Bake at 350° for 1 hour. Great served with rice.

Peachy Mustard Pork Chops

4 (4-ounce) thick boneless center-cut pork chops
½ teaspoon salt
½ cup peach preserves
2 tablespoons Dijon mustard
1 tablespoon water

Sprinkle chops with salt. Spray a 10-inch skillet with nonstick cooking spray. Over medium-high heat, cook chops 2 minutes on each side. Reduce heat to medium, and cook 5 minutes more on each side. Combine peach preserves, mustard, and water; stir well. Pour sauce over chops, and cook till heated through, 2–3 minutes. Serve sauce over chops. Sprinkle with pepper, if desired.

Tex Mex Chops

6 pork chops
1 (15-ounce) can hot chili beans
1½ cups salsa
1 (8-ounce) can shoe peg corn, drained
2 cups cooked rice

Place pork chops in crockpot. Add beans and salsa. Cover, and cook on HIGH 2½ hours. Stir in corn. Cover and cook 30 minutes longer. Serve over hot cooked rice.

Potato Crusted Pork Cutlets

2 tablespoons mustard
2 eggs, beaten
2½ pounds pork cutlets
1 cup instant mashed potato flakes
¼ cup oil

Stir together mustard and eggs. Coat cutlets with egg mixture, then potato flakes. Cook in hot oil in a large skillet about 10 minutes on each side, or till done. Season with salt and pepper to taste.

Last Minute Ham Casserole

1 cup chopped ham
1 tablespoon dried onion flakes
2 eggs, beaten
¾ cup milk
¾ cup biscuit mix

Combine all ingredients; add salt and pepper to taste. Pour into greased 2-quart casserole and bake at 350° for 30 minutes.

Yankee Stadium, which opened in April 1923 in the Bronx, New York, was built on a **five**-sided, irregular plot of land. This gave it a very distinctive asymmetrical shape. At the time the stadium was built, there was media discussion over the short right field line (295 feet), which clearly favored left-handed power hitters such as the Yankees' rising star, Babe Ruth. For many years, and even today after remodeling, left field and center field were and are much more difficult areas to hit home runs than right field.

Ham and Cheese Fold-Over Pizzas

1 (10-ounce) package refrigerated pizza dough
¼ cup Dijon mustard
1 (8-ounce) package shredded Swiss cheese, divided
1½ cups diced cooked ham
½ teaspoon caraway seeds

Preheat oven to 400°. On a floured surface, roll dough into a 10x15-inch rectangle. Cut dough into 4 rectangles. Spread mustard over rectangles. Divide half the cheese among the rectangles diagonally, placing cheese only on triangle half of each. Sprinkle ham and caraway seeds over cheese. Top with remaining cheese. Brush edges with water, then fold over and seal edges with fork. Place on greased baking sheet. Prick tops so steam can escape. Bake 15–20 minutes or until done. Serves 4.

Glazed Ham Steak

1 (6- to 8-ounce) ham steak
½ (8-ounce) jar apricot preserves
¼ cup brown sugar
¼ cup orange juice
1 tablespoon cornstarch

In large skillet coated with nonstick spray, heat ham steak on medium-high heat until hot. Add apricot preserves and brown sugar, coating ham steak. Mix orange juice with cornstarch; pour over all. Reduce heat and simmer 5–6 minutes. Stir glaze till clear and slightly thickened. Remove ham steak and continue to heat till glaze thickens. Serve glaze over ham steaks.

Lemony Sweet Ham

¹/₂ lemon
²/₃ cup brown sugar
1 tablespoon mustard
¹/₈ teaspoon ground cloves
1 thick ham slice

Preheat broiler. Zest lemon half in small bowl, then squeeze juice over zest. Mix in brown sugar, mustard, and cloves. Broil ham slice 4 inches from heat for 5 minutes, then turn and top with sauce. Broil 3 more minutes, or until sauce bubbles. Serves 2.

Dinner in a Pumpkin Shell

1 (12-inch) pumpkin
1 pound bulk pork sausage
1 cup rice, cooked
1 (4-ounce) can sliced mushrooms, drained
1 (10³/₄-ounce) can cream of mushroom soup

Cut a large lid from top of pumpkin. Scoop out seeds and strings, and wash the pumpkin inside and out. Brown sausage in large skillet, then drain. Add rice, mushrooms, and soup, and stir well. Pour into pumpkin shell, and replace "lid." Put pumpkin in large roasting pan, along with 1½–2 cups water. Bake at 350° for 2 hours. Remove "lid" and spoon out from top of pumpkin. If desired, cut squares of pumpkin from opening down, and serve with sausage-rice mixture. Serves 6.

Grilled Cabbage Packets

3 cups purchased coleslaw mix
⅓ cup zesty Italian salad dressing
½ cup chopped red bell pepper
½ cup chopped red onion
1 pound polish sausages, fully cooked,
    cut into 4 equal lengths

Combine coleslaw mix, salad dressing, bell pepper, and onion, and mix gently. Place sausages in large square of aluminum foil, and top with coleslaw mix. Cover with foil, completely sealing edges. Grill over medium heat 15–20 minutes, until heated through. Serves 4.

French Fried Hot Dog

1 cup French fried onions
8 beef hot dogs
8 hot dog buns, split
¼ cup mustard hot dog relish
¼ cup French salad dressing

In 8-inch nonstick skillet, cook onions over medium-high heat, stirring occasionally, about 5 minutes. Set aside. Cut hot dogs in half lengthwise, cutting almost, but not completely through. Open and place cut side down on grill. Cook over medium heat about 7 minutes or until thoroughly heated, turning once. Grill hot dog buns, cut side down, during last 2 minutes. Spread cut side of each bun with relish. Place hot dog in each bun; top with French dressing and French fried onions.

Nacho Dogs

1 cup crushed Doritos
1 package jumbo hot dogs, chopped
½ cup mild salsa
1 (10¾-ounce) can fiesta nacho cheese soup
½ cup shredded Cheddar cheese

Place Doritos in bottom of small baking dish. Brown hot dogs in nonstick skillet over medium-high heat. When browned, stir in salsa and soup. Heat through. Pour over Doritos, then sprinkle with cheese. Bake at 350° about 30 minutes.

Fried Liver and Onions in Gravy

½ pound bacon
1 pound onions, sliced
1 pound baby beef liver
1 cup all-purpose flour
1½ cups beef broth

Preheat oven to 200°. Fry bacon and drain, reserving bacon grease. Keep bacon warm in oven.

Return 2 tablespoons grease to same skillet, and on medium-high heat, sauté onions till translucent; add more bacon grease 1 tablespoon at a time, if needed. Remove onions to oven to keep warm.

Return remaining bacon grease to skillet. Coat liver in flour, and sear in skillet over medium-high heat; watch carefully. As soon as liquid seeps to top of meat, turn and cook 2 minutes on other side. Remove meat to oven to keep warm.

Sprinkle remaining flour into hot skillet, and stir constantly until flour begins to brown, then add broth. Boil for 1 minute, then reduce heat and simmer 1 minute longer. Pour gravy over liver and onions, and sprinkle crumbled bacon on top.

The year **1905** is referred to as an *annus mirabilis* ("wonderful year" or "year of wonders") because of the publication of several papers by Albert Einstein that lay the foundations for quantum physics, which introduced the special theory of relativity, explained Brownian motion, and proved the existence of atoms.

Lovely Lamb in French Ginger Marinade

1 cup French salad dressing
1½ cups sliced onions
2 cloves garlic, minced
1 teaspoon grated ginger
1 (5-pound) leg of lamb

Combine dressing, onions, garlic, and ginger. Pour over leg of lamb. Refrigerate 6 hours or overnight, turning occasionally. Drain and reserve marinade.

Place lamb on a rack in a roasting pan. Insert meat thermometer into the thickest part of meat, making sure not to touch bone. Bake 2½ hours in 350° oven or until meat thermometer registers 180°, basting occasionally with marinade during cooking. Serves 6–8.

Fast
and
Fabulous

FIVE ★ STAR

Poultry

Fried Beer-Battered Chicken Strips

1½ pounds boneless, skinless chicken breast halves
1½ cups all-purpose flour, divided
1 teaspoon baking powder
½ cup cold beer
2 eggs, beaten

Wash chicken. Cut chicken lengthwise into 1-inch-wide strips. Place ½ cup flour in a small bowl. Place remaining flour in medium bowl along with baking powder; stir in beer and eggs to form a batter. Dredge chicken strips in flour, then in batter. Deep-fry a few at a time in hot oil, turning to evenly brown on all sides. Salt and pepper to taste. Keep warm until serving.

Fried Buttermilk Chicken

2 eggs
3 cups buttermilk
8 boneless, skinless chicken breast halves,
    cut in 3 strips
1–2 teaspoons salt
1½ cups self-rising flour

In a large bowl, beat eggs and buttermilk. Add chicken and refrigerate about 30 minutes or more.

Remove chicken from milk mixture; season well with salt. Flour chicken one piece at a time. Deep-fry chicken in hot oil till golden brown. Season to taste with salt and pepper.

5

Spicy Oven Fried Chicken

The taste will amaze you!

½ cup buttermilk
¼ cup hot sauce
1 cup finely crushed cornflakes
½ cup all-purpose flour
6 boneless, skinless chicken breast halves

Mix buttermilk and hot sauce in medium bowl. Mix cornflakes and flour in a separate bowl. Dip chicken breasts, one at a time, in buttermilk mixture. Season with salt and pepper to taste, then roll in cornflake mixture. Place on a greased baking pan in a single layer. Drizzle a small amount of oil over chicken, if desired. Bake at 375° for 30 minutes, turning once.

Spicy Fried Drumsticks

8 chicken legs, skin removed
¼ cup hot sauce
⅓ cup all-purpose flour
2 tablespoons yellow cornmeal
½ teaspoon salt

Wash chicken. Place in large zipper bag. Pour hot sauce over chicken. Seal bag and marinate in fridge for 1 hour, or longer. (The longer it marinates, the spicier it is.)

In a separate large zipper bag, combine flour, cornmeal, and salt. Add marinated chicken, seal, and shake to coat. Deep-fry in hot oil about 15 minutes, or until done.

Water is the source of all life on earth. The distribution of water, however, is quite varied; many locations have plenty of it while others have very little. Water exists on earth as a solid (ice), liquid, or gas (water vapor). Despite continual movement within the hydrosphere, the total amount of water at any one time remains essentially constant.

The continuous movement of water on, above, and below the surface of the earth is known as the hydrologic or water cycle. The water cycle has **five** main physical processes:

- evaporation
- condensation
- precipitation
- infiltration
- surface run-off

Did you know there are **five-leaf clovers**? The **five-leaf clover** is a mutation (like the four-leaf clover) that does appear occasionally, but less common than the four-leaf clover. The superstition for the **five-leaf clover** is extra good luck and attracting money.

Fast and Fabulous Crusty Chicken for Two

6 chicken breast strips
2 tablespoons milk or cream
8 single Waverly crackers, crumbled
2 tablespoons seasoned flour
2 tablespoons olive oil

Wash and paper towel dry chicken strips; lay in a shallow bowl in milk. Mix cracker crumbs with flour in another shallow bowl. Heat olive oil in skillet on medium-high heat. Dip wet chicken quickly on both sides in crumb mixture. Place in hot oil and pan-fry for about 3 minutes on each side, till browned and cooked through.

Editor's Extra: Seasoning can vary. Mrs. Dash Spicy Seasoning is great, and so is Cajun or Greek seasoning.

Sesame Chicken Nuggets

4 boneless, skinless chicken breast halves
¼ cup toasted sesame seeds
2 tablespoons all-purpose flour
2 tablespoons soy sauce
2 tablespoons butter, melted

Preheat oven to 400°. Wash chicken, and cut each piece into fourths. Sprinkle with salt and pepper to taste. In a shallow bowl, combine sesame seeds and flour. Place soy sauce in a separate bowl. Lightly grease a baking pan with sides. Dip chicken pieces in soy sauce to coat, then dredge in flour mixture. Place on baking pan in a single layer. Drizzle with melted butter. Bake at 400° for 25–30 minutes, or until done.

Hidden Valley Chicken Strips

2 cups crushed cornflakes
2 tablespoons chopped fresh basil, or 1 teaspoon
crushed dried basil
1 (8-ounce) bottle Hidden Valley Ranch Dressing,
divided
4 boneless skinless chicken breast halves, cut into
thin strips
½ teaspoon freshly ground black pepper

Preheat oven to 425°. Combine cornflakes and basil in a medium bowl. Put ½ bottle dressing in a separate bowl. Dip chicken strips in dressing, sprinkle with pepper, and coat in cornflake mixture. Arrange chicken in a single layer on nonstick baking pan, and bake 15 minutes, or until done. Use remaining dressing as a dip.

Peanut Chicken Tenders

½ cup finely chopped peanuts or nut topping
½ cup fine dry bread crumbs
½ teaspoon crushed red pepper flakes
1 package chicken tenders, uncooked, rinsed,
patted dry
1 stick butter, melted

Mix peanuts, bread crumbs, and red pepper flakes in a small bowl. Dip chicken tenders in melted butter, then in breading mixture. Spray a cookie sheet or shallow baking pan with cooking spray. Lay breaded chicken tenders on cookie sheet. Bake at 375° about 25 minutes or until juices run clear and breading is crispy on chicken. Serve warm with your favorite dipping sauce, or on top of your favorite green salad.

Classic Chicken Casserole

1 (3-ounce) jar dried beef
4 boneless chicken breast halves
4 slices bacon
1 cup sour cream
1 (10¾-ounce) can cream of mushroom soup

Preheat oven to 350°. Tear dried beef into small pieces and put in bottom of 2-quart casserole dish. Lay breasts on top, then bacon slices. Mix sour cream and soup, and pour over chicken. Bake 55 minutes.

Easy Chicken Cordon Bleu

8 skinless, boneless chicken breast halves
½ teaspoon salt
12 slices Swiss cheese, divided
8 slices cooked ham
1 cup seasoned bread crumbs

Preheat oven to 350°. Grease a 9x13-inch baking dish. Flatten chicken breasts to ¼-inch thickness. Season chicken with salt. Place 1 slice Swiss cheese and 1 slice ham on top of each breast. Roll up, and secure with a toothpick. Place in baking dish, and sprinkle evenly with bread crumbs. Bake about 35 minutes, or until chicken is no longer pink. Remove from oven; top with remaining 4 slices of halved cheese. Return to oven 5 more minutes to melt cheese. Remove toothpicks before serving.

Skillet Chicken Prosciutto

4 boneless, skinless chicken breast halves
4 thin slices prosciutto
⅓ cup butter
1 cup white wine
4 slices provolone cheese

Wash chicken. Pound to ¼-inch thickness. Place 1 prosciutto slice over each chicken breast and secure with toothpicks. Melt butter in 10-inch nonstick skillet over medium-high heat. Cook chicken on one side about 5 minutes, or until almost cooked through. Pour wine over chicken, and cook until evaporated. Put 1 slice cheese over each ham slice, and cover skillet to allow cheese to melt.

Creamy Delicious Chicken Breasts

8 chicken breast halves
8 slices Swiss cheese
1 (10¾-ounce) can cream of chicken soup
1 cup crushed herb-seasoned croutons
¼ cup butter, melted

Place chicken in greased baking dish. Top with Swiss cheese, then soup. Sprinkle with croutons. Drizzle with melted butter. Bake uncovered at 350° about 45 minutes.

The Chinese Zodiac is based on a twelve-year cycle, and each year represented by an animal.

The Dragon is the **fifth** sign of the Chinese Zodiac. It is the only mythical animal in the zodiac, and is associated with strength, health, harmony, and good luck. Dragons are placed above doors or on the tops of roofs to banish demons and evil spirits. Within Chinese cultures, more babies are born in Dragon years than in any other animal years. Recent Dragon years are 1952, 1964, 1976, 1980, and 2000.

Some famous people born in the year of the Dragon:

- Abraham Lincoln
- John Lennon
- Julius Caesar
- Martin Luther King Jr.
- Napoleon III of France
- Pelé
- Plácido Domingo
- Rasputin
- Vladimir Putin

Weighing **five** grams, the United States **five-cent** coin is a unit of currency equaling **five** hundredths of a United States dollar. Prior to introduction of the **nickel**, **five-cent** pieces were very small silver coins called half dimes. Due to short-ages of silver during and after the Civil War, an alternative metal was needed for **five-cent** coinage, and the cop-per-nickel alloy still in use today was selected.

The **nickel's** design since 1938 has featured a profile of President Thomas Jefferson. From 1938 to 2003, Monticello was featured on the reverse. For 2004 and 2005, **nickels** featured new designs to commemorate the bicentennials of the Louisiana Purchase and the Lewis and Clark expedition; these new designs were called the Westward Journey **nickel** series. In 2006, Monticello returned to the reverse, while a new image of Jefferson facing forward was fea-tured on the obverse.

Chicken in the Ritz

2 eggs
1 cup crushed Ritz Crackers
½ teaspoon garlic salt
4 boneless, skinless chicken breast halves
1 stick butter, melted

Preheat oven to 375°. Place eggs in a bowl, and beat until frothy. Place cracker crumbs and garlic salt in a separate bowl; mix together. Wash chicken, and sea-son with black pepper to taste. Dip chicken in eggs, then coat with cracker crumbs. Arrange coated chick-en in a lightly greased 2-quart baking dish. Drizzle with butter. Bake 35–40 minutes, or until chicken is done.

Easy Cheesy Chicken

4 boneless, skinless chicken breast halves
2 (10¾-ounce) cans condensed cream of chicken soup
¼ cup mayonnaise
1 teaspoon curry powder
½ cup freshly grated Parmesan cheese

Wash chicken and pat dry. Preheat oven to 350°. Place chicken in a 9x13-inch baking dish. Combine remaining ingredients, and pour over chicken. Cover and bake in 350° oven 35–40 minutes, or until chicken is done. Remove cover during last 10 minutes of cook time.

2006 U.S. nickel design

Cheezy Chicken

4 chicken breast halves
1 teaspoon salt
1 teaspoon black pepper
1/2 box Cheese Nips, crushed
1/2–1 stick butter

Sprinkle chicken breasts with salt and pepper. Place crushed Cheese Nips in bowl large enough to hold chicken breasts. Toss to coat. Melt butter in oven-proof baking dish and place chicken breasts skin side down; cover with foil. Place in cold oven, turn heat to 325°, and bake 1 hour. Remove foil, turn chicken over, and cook another 15–20 minutes.

Chicken with Lime Butter

6 boneless, skinless chicken breast halves
4 tablespoons vegetable oil
1 lime, juiced
1/2 cup butter
1/2 teaspoon dried dill weed

Wash chicken, pat dry, and, if desired, season with salt and pepper to taste. In 10-inch skillet over medium-high heat, heat oil and cook chicken until lightly browned, about 3 minutes on each side. Reduce heat to low. Cover, and cook until no longer pink, about 10 minutes. Remove from pan, and keep warm.

Wipe excess oil from pan. Stir in lime juice, and bring to a boil over medium-high heat. Gradually stir in butter, 1 tablespoon at a time. Continue stirring until sauce thickens. Remove from heat, and stir in dill weed. Spoon sauce over chicken, and serve.

Savory Cashew Chicken

1 (12-ounce) jar apricot preserves
¼ cup Dijon mustard
1 teaspoon curry powder
1 cup chopped cashews
4 boneless, skinless chicken breast halves

Preheat oven to 375°. Combine preserves, mustard, and curry powder in a large skillet. Cook over low heat, stirring constantly, until preserves are completely melted. Put cashews in small bowl. Coat chicken in sauce, then roll in nuts. Bake in a greased 9x13-inch baking dish at 375° for 25–30 minutes. Just before serving time, bring remaining sauce to a boil, then lower heat and cook for 2 minutes. Serve over baked chicken.

Colorful Stir-Fry Chicken

4 chicken tenders, cut into chunks
1 teaspoon Greek seasoning
1 cup frozen seasoning blend
6 mushrooms, sliced
2 tablespoons soy sauce

Sprinkle chicken pieces with Greek seasoning. Cook in skillet with a small amount of oil about 5 minutes, turning often. Add seasoning blend, mushrooms, and soy sauce. Cook on medium-high heat 5–10 minutes, tossing to distribute soy sauce over all. May serve over rice or noodles, if desired. Serves 2.

Editor's Extra: If you can't find frozen seasoning blend in the frozen vegetable section of your grocery store, you can make up your own mix of chopped onions, bell peppers, celery, and parsley.

Lemon Broiled Honey Dijon Chicken

Quick and delicious! Always a hit.

4 boneless, skinless chicken breast halves
¼ cup lemon juice
2 tablespoons oil
2 tablespoons honey
2 tablespoons Dijon mustard

Wash and dry chicken, then marinate in remaining ingredients, covered, in refrigerator about 20 minutes or more.

Place chicken in baking pan and broil 4–6 inches from broiler about 8–12 minutes; turn and spoon additional marinade on top. Broil another 8–10 minutes till slightly brown on top and juices run clear. Serves 4.

Editor's Extra: If chicken becomes dry, heat a little honey Dijon salad dressing and spoon on top.

Honey Mustard Chicken

6 boneless, skinless chicken breast halves
½ cup prepared mustard
½ cup honey
1 teaspoon paprika
1 teaspoon dried basil

Preheat oven to 350°. Place chicken in greased 9x13-inch baking dish. Combine mustard, honey, paprika, and basil. Mix well. Spread chicken with ½ the honey mustard sauce. Bake 30 minutes. Turn chicken over, and spread with remaining ½ of honey mustard sauce. Bake 10 more minutes, or until chicken is done.

Humans are **pentadactyl**, as are all primates. **Pentadactyly** is the condition of having **five** digits (fingers and toes) on each limb. Furthermore, it is believed that all land vertebrates are believed to have descended from an ancestor with a **pentadactyl** limb, although many groups of species have lost or transformed some or all of their digits. This phenomenon is featured in the work of Charles Darwin.

Honey-Glazed Chicken Legs

1 tablespoon chili powder
1 tablespoon honey
1 tablespoon lime juice
½ teaspoon black pepper
2 pounds drumsticks

Preheat oven to 425°. Combine chili powder, honey, lime juice, and pepper in a large bowl. Add drumsticks, and coat well. Place chicken in roasting pan lined with foil. Cook 30–35 minutes, or until cooked through, turning once during cook time.

Dandy Garlic Chicken

4 boneless, skinless chicken breast halves
2 teaspoons garlic powder
1 teaspoon seasoning salt
1 teaspoon onion powder
3 tablespoons butter

Wash chicken and pat dry. Sprinkle with garlic powder, seasoning salt, and onion powder. In a large skillet over medium-high heat, melt butter. Add chicken and sauté about 15 minutes on each side, or until chicken is done.

Speedy Herbed Chicken

4 boneless, skinless chicken breast halves
1 stick butter, softened
¼ teaspoon dried rosemary
3 cloves garlic, minced
¼ teaspoon dried thyme

Preheat oven to broil. Line baking pan with aluminum foil. Combine butter, rosemary, garlic, and thyme. Place chicken in pan, then spread butter mixture evenly over chicken. Broil in preheated oven, basting frequently with remaining butter mixture about 15 minutes or until chicken is done.

Savory Baked Chicken

4 skinless, boneless chicken breast halves
2 medium onions, sliced into rings
1 head garlic, peeled, sliced
¼ cup fresh lemon juice
½ cup white wine

Wash chicken. Preheat oven to 350°. Lightly grease a medium baking dish. Layer bottom of baking dish with ½ the onions and ½ the garlic slices. Pour lemon juice and white wine into baking dish. Season chicken with salt and pepper to taste, and place in baking dish. Top with remaining onions and garlic. Bake 25 minutes in preheated oven, or until chicken juices run clear.

Lemon Baked Chicken

1 fryer, cut in pieces
¼ cup butter, melted
2 tablespoons lemon juice
1 teaspoon dried tarragon
¼ teaspoon cracked black pepper

Place chicken in shallow baking dish. Mix remaining ingredients together. Brush chicken thoroughly with butter mixture. Bake in 350° oven 1 hour, or until tender, basting occasionally. Serves 4–6.

Quick & Easy Coca-Cola Chicken

1 large fryer, cut up
½ teaspoon garlic powder
1 cup ketchup
1 cup Coca-Cola
1 tablespoon Worcestershire

Wash chicken, and pat dry. Season with garlic powder, and salt and pepper to taste. Place in large frying pan. Combine ketchup, Coca-Cola, and Worcestershire, and pour over chicken. Simmer, covered, 55–60 minutes, turning once. Serve with rice.

Italian Chicken

4 boneless, skinless chicken breast halves
2 (14½-ounce) cans Italian-style stewed tomatoes
½ teaspoon oregano
2 tablespoons cornstarch
¼ cup grated Parmesan cheese

Preheat oven to 425°. Wash chicken, and place in lightly greased 2-quart baking dish. Cover dish with foil, and bake 15 minutes in preheated oven; drain juices.

In saucepan, combine tomatoes, oregano, and cornstarch, and cook until thickened. Pour sauce over chicken, then top with Parmesan cheese. Bake until chicken is done, about 10 minutes.

Editor's Extra: Add a few dashes hot pepper sauce to jazz it up a bit.

Chicken and Artichokes

4 boneless, skinless chicken breast halves
2 teaspoons olive oil
1 (14½-ounce) can diced tomatoes with green peppers and onions
¼ cup sun-dried tomato pesto
1 (14-ounce) can artichoke hearts in water, drained, quartered

Wash chicken, then sprinkle with salt and pepper to taste. In a large skillet over medium-high heat, heat olive oil, and cook chicken on both sides till nearly done. Remove chicken from pan, and set aside.

In same pan, cook tomatoes for 1 minute, stirring constantly. Add pesto, artichokes, and chicken. Cover, and reduce heat. Simmer 5–10 minutes, or until chicken is done.

Honey Baked Chicken Cubes

4 boneless, skinless chicken breast halves, cubed
¾ cup honey, divided
½ cup Worcestershire
½ teaspoon salt
¼ teaspoon pepper

Combine chicken cubes, ½ cup honey, Worcestershire, salt, and pepper in a greased 2-quart baking dish. Let marinate about 10 minutes while oven is preheating to 400°. Bake chicken 20 minutes, stirring occasionally to prevent sticking. Drain juices, then add remaining honey. Continue cooking until sauce thickens.

Marmalade BBQ Chicken

2 pounds boneless, skinless chicken
⅓ cup orange marmalade
⅓ cup spicy barbecue sauce
2 tablespoons Worcestershire
2 tablespoons lemon juice

Wash chicken, and pat dry. Sprinkle with salt and pepper, if desired. Place in well-greased 9x13-inch pan. Blend together marmalade, barbecue sauce, Worcestershire, and lemon juice. Pour sauce over chicken and bake at 350° about 45 minutes, or till done.

Fifth Avenue is a major thoroughfare in the center of the borough of Manhattan in New York City. It runs through the heart of Midtown and along the eastern side of Central Park, and because of the expensive park-view real estate and historical mansions along its course, it is a symbol of wealthy New York. It is one of the best shopping streets in the world, like London's Oxford Street and the Champs Elysées in Paris.

Lemonade Chicken

1 (6-ounce) can frozen lemonade concentrate, thawed
⅓ cup soy sauce
½ teaspoon celery salt
⅛ teaspoon garlic powder
5 pounds cut-up chicken, skin removed

In a medium bowl, blend together lemonade concentrate, soy sauce, celery salt, and garlic powder. Dip chicken pieces in sauce, and place in greased 9x13-inch baking dish. Bake in 350° oven about 60 minutes, basting occasionally throughout cooking time.

Peachy Chicken

8 boneless, skinless chicken breast halves
1 cup brown sugar, divided
1 (29-ounce) can peaches, or 4 fresh peaches, peeled, pitted, sliced
⅛ teaspoon ground cloves
2 tablespoons fresh lemon juice

Preheat oven to 350°. Lightly grease a 9x13-inch baking dish. Place chicken in prepared baking dish, and sprinkle with ½ cup brown sugar. Arrange peach slices over chicken, then sprinkle with remaining ½ cup brown sugar, cloves, and lemon juice. Bake about 30–40 minutes, basting often with juices.

Baked Oriental Chicken

6 boneless, skinless chicken breast halves
1 cup soy sauce
½ cup vinegar
1 cup chopped green bell pepper
2 (8-ounce) cans sliced water chestnuts, drained

Preheat oven to 350°. Wash chicken, and place in a greased 9x13-inch baking dish. Combine soy sauce and vinegar; pour over chicken. Sprinkle with water chestnuts. Bake 40 minutes, or until chicken is cooked through.

Grilled Teriyaki Chicken

4 boneless, skinless chicken breast halves
1 cup teriyaki sauce
¼ cup lemon juice
2 teaspoons minced garlic
2 teaspoons sesame oil

Marinate chicken in mixture of teriyaki sauce, lemon juice, garlic, and sesame oil for 24 hours, turning occasionally.

Grill chicken over high heat 6–8 minutes on each side, or until done.

Oriental Chicken Wings

These are soooo good!

½ cup brown sugar
½ cup soy sauce
½ cup water
2 garlic cloves, minced
2½ pounds chicken wings

Preheat oven to 350°. Place chicken wings in a greased 9x13-inch baking dish. Combine sugar, soy sauce, water, and garlic, and pour over chicken. Bake 1½ hours, basting occasionally.

Chicken and Rice Casserole

1 envelope dry onion soup mix
1 (10¾-ounce) can cream of mushroom soup
2¼ cups water
1 cup rice, uncooked
1 whole chicken, cut up

Preheat oven to 350°. Blend onion soup mix with mushroom soup and water. Place rice in a lightly greased 9x13-inch baking pan, and pour ½ soup mixture over. Place chicken on rice skin side up. Season with salt and pepper to taste, then cover with remaining soup mixture. Cover with foil, and bake in 350° oven till done, 60–70 minutes. Remove cover during last 20 minutes to brown chicken.

Chicken and Rice Medley

1 (5.6-ounce) package Lipton Rice Medley
1 (10-ounce) package frozen broccoli in butter sauce
1 cup prepared Alfredo sauce
2 cups cooked cubed cooked chicken
1 cup grated Parmesan cheese

Cook rice medley according to package directions. Cook broccoli according to package directions. Spread rice medley in bottom of lightly greased 2-quart baking dish. Cover with broccoli, then chicken, then Alfredo sauce; sprinkle with Parmesan. Bake in 350° oven for 30 minutes, or until heated through. Serves 4.

5

Good As Mama's Chicken Pie

2 skinless, boneless chicken breast halves
2 (10¾-ounce) cans cream of chicken soup
½–¾ cup water
1 (10-ounce) package frozen stew vegetables
Pie crust for 2 pies (refrigerated roll-up crust works
    well)

Boil chicken breasts in seasoned water, cut into cubes. Combine chicken cubes, soup, water (to desired consistency), and stew vegetables. Put one pie crust in greased 2-quart casserole dish and prick with a fork. Prebake at 400° for 15 minutes. Place chicken mixture in crust and place second crust on top; prick. Bake in 350° oven 40–45 minutes. May cover top with foil during last few minutes to keep from browning too much.

Editor's Extra: A can of drained English peas may be added to chicken mixture, if desired.

Cheesy Chicken Crescents

8 boneless, skinless chicken breast halves
2 (10¾-ounce) cans condensed cream of chicken soup
2½ cups milk
1½ cups shredded Cheddar cheese, divided
2 (8-count) cans crescent rolls

Boil or bake chicken till done. Cut into cubes. In saucepan over medium-low heat, heat soup, milk, and 1 cup cheese until cheese is melted; stir to blend. Pour ½ of soup mixture into lightly greased 9x13-inch baking dish.

Separate crescent rolls into triangles. Place some chicken onto large end of crescent, and top with a sprinkle of cheese. Roll up and place in soup mixture. Bake at 350° for 10–15 minutes, until crescents are lightly browned. Pour remaining soup mixture over crescents, and sprinkle any leftover chicken and/or cheese over top. Return to oven until rolls are browned.

Chicken Croquettes

2 cups chopped onions
3 cups chopped cooked chicken
1½ cups seasoned bread crumbs
3 eggs, lightly beaten
1 tablespoon chopped fresh parsley

Sauté onions. Combine with chicken, bread crumbs, and eggs; mix well. Add parsley, and if desired, salt and pepper to taste; mix well. With hand, form mixture into small patties. Fry patties in small amount of oil over medium heat until golden brown.

Barbecued Chicken Sandwiches

1 pound ground chicken
1 tablespoon oil
1 cup barbecue sauce
2 teaspoons chili powder
4 hamburger buns (with sesame seeds)

In a medium skillet, heat oil. Add ground chicken and cook till done. Stir in barbecue sauce and chili powder, and simmer 5 minutes. Toast buns. Serve in buns.

Cheesy Chicken Nachos

1½ cups cubed cooked chicken
¾ cup spicy barbecue sauce
8 cups tortilla chips
1½ cups seeded and chopped tomatoes
3 cups shredded Colby-Jack cheese

Preheat oven to 350°. Combine chicken and barbecue sauce in a small bowl. Spray 2 large rectangles of heavy-duty foil with nonstick cooking spray. Spread tortilla chips down center of foil. Top with chicken mixture, tomatoes, and cheese. Seal packages with double fold. Bake 4–6 inches from heat source for 8–10 minutes, until hot, and cheese is melted. Serves 8.

Mexican Chicken

4 boneless, skinless chicken breast halves
2 tablespoons taco seasoning
1 cup salsa, divided
1 avocado, pitted, peeled, sliced
1 cup shredded Cheddar cheese

Preheat oven to 400°. Season chicken with taco seasoning. Bake uncovered in greased 2-quart casserole dish for 20 minutes. Spoon ½ cup salsa evenly over chicken. Bake, uncovered, for 15 minutes. Remove from oven, and top with remaining salsa, avocado slices, and cheese. Bake, uncovered, 5 more minutes.

Southwestern Chicken Quiche

1 (9-inch) deep-dish pie crust
4 large eggs
1 cup half-and-half
1 cup cubed cooked southwestern-flavored chicken
½ cup finely chopped onion

Bake pie crust at 400° for 5 minutes; set aside. Combine eggs, half-and-half, cubed chicken, and onion; mix well. Pour into prebaked pie crust; bake at 350° for 40–45 minutes. Serves 8.

Quick Alfredo Pizza

1 cup Alfredo sauce, or to taste
1 (6-ounce) package cooked bacon pieces
2 (6-ounce) packages cooked chicken strips
1–1½ cups shredded mozzarella cheese
1 prepared pizza crust, or make your own

Layer pizza ingredients on top of pizza crust in the order above. Bake at 375° for 15–20 minutes, or until cheese browns on top.

In ancient and medieval natural philosophy, **quintessence**, meaning "**fifth element**," refers to the elusive **fifth** element that completes the basic four elements (water, fire, air, and earth)—thought to be the material of the stars, forming heavenly bodies, and pervading all things.

Quintessence and the corresponding adjective **quintessential** are also used in the figurative sense—something that is the perfect example of its kind.

The Fifth Element (1997), a science fiction movie starring Bruce Willis and Milla Jovovich, places the survival of mankind on the shoulders of Korben Dallas (Willis) after "the **fifth element** (Jovovich)" falls into his taxicab. His mission is to find the other four elements. The **five** elements together will produce the Divine Light, which vanquishes the Ultimate Evil for another **five thousand** years.

Henry Ford is said to have paid his assembly-line workers an unheard of **$5.00** a day in 1914— twice the usual manufacturing wage at the time. This attracted the best workers.

Ford was also the first to build factories around the concept of the assembly line. It usually consists of each worker in control of one specific job, and their work-related movements are reduced to a minimum.

This method of construction allows a faster and more cost-effective method of producing vehicles. Parts of a product are pieced together by individual workers. As a result, Henry Ford's cars came off the assembly line in 3-minute intervals, a speed much faster than previous methods.

The combination of high wages and high efficiency was copied by most major industries and is still used today.

Turkey Tortillas

6 (8-inch) flour tortillas
6 tablespoons ranch salad dressing
2 cups cubed cooked turkey breast, or 2 (5-ounce) cans chunk-style turkey, drained
2 avocados, peeled, pitted, sliced
1½ cups shredded Monterey Jack cheese

Spread each tortilla with 1 tablespoon salad dressing. Place turkey and avocado slices over ½ of each tortilla, then sprinkle with cheese. Fold in half, and cook over medium heat in large nonstick skillet a couple minutes on each side, till lightly browned. Serves 6.

Grilled Turkey Burgers

1 pound ground turkey
4 hamburger buns, split
¼ cup basil pesto
4 slices provolone cheese
1 large tomato, sliced

Form ground turkey into 4 flat patties, seasoning with salt and pepper, if desired. Grill over medium-high heat till done. When done, put burgers on buns, and top with pesto and a slice of cheese. Put back on grill till cheese melts, about 1 minute. Top each burger with a slice of tomato.

1913 Ford assembly line

178

5

Marinated Turkey Breast

1 turkey breast
2 cups Sauterne
1 cup oil
1 cup soy sauce
1 clove garlic, minced

Wash turkey and pat dry. Slice into 8 fillets. In a large bowl, mix wine, oil, soy sauce, and garlic. Marinate turkey in mixture, covered, overnight.

Grill over hot coals about 45 minutes, turning occasionally. Serves 6–8.

Slow-Cooked Turkey and Stuffing

1 cup chopped onion
2 tablespoons apple jelly
1 (6-ounce) package turkey-flavored stuffing mix
¾ cup water
2 pounds boneless, skinless turkey breast

Sauté onion in large nonstick skillet. Add jelly and stir to combine. Place stuffing mix in crockpot. Add water and mix. Season turkey with salt and pepper to taste. Place on top of stuffing mix. Spread onion mixture evenly over turkey. Cover and cook on LOW 5–6 hours.

Smothered Quail with Pan Gravy

8 quail breasts
¾ cup plus 1 tablespoon all-purpose flour, divided
1 stick butter
½ cup chicken broth
¼ cup chopped parsley

Wash quail, and sprinkle with salt and pepper, if desired. Add ¾ cup flour to large zipper bag. Add quail, close zipper, and shake to coat. Melt butter in large skillet over medium heat. Add quail, and cook on both sides until browned. Add chicken broth to skillet. Cover, and cook about 15 minutes longer. Remove from pan and keep warm. To remaining 1 tablespoon flour, add about 2 tablespoons pan juices; stir to dissolve. Add to remaining pan juices, and cook until thickened. Serve gravy over quail. Garnish with parsley. Serves 4.

White Barbecue Sauce

½ cup mayonnaise
¼ cup apple cider vinegar
Salt and pepper to taste
¼ teaspoon cayenne pepper
2 tablespoons apple juice

Mix together, and serve on buns with breaded chicken cutlets and your favorite garnishes.

Fast
and
Fabulous

FIVE ★ STAR

Seafood

Fish Fillet Dogs

1 (11.4-ounce) package crunchy golden fish fillets
½ cup mayonnaise or salad dressing
¼ cup grated Parmesan cheese
¼ teaspoon garlic powder
3 hot dog buns

Preheat oven to 400°. Place frozen fish fillets in jelly-roll pan and bake 15 minutes. Meanwhile, mix mayonnaise, cheese, and garlic powder; spread on cut side of buns. When fish are done, place buns, cut side up, in same pan with fish. Bake 8–10 more minutes. Place fillets between buns.

Editor's Extra: May serve with sliced tomato, bell pepper slices, sweet pickles, dill relish, etc.

Grilled Bacon-Wrapped Fish with Herbs

4 (1-pound) whole fish, cleaned
1 teaspoon salt
1 cup fresh herbs
1 tablespoon olive oil
4–8 thin slices bacon

Rinse fish; pat dry. Sprinkle with salt. Place fresh herbs inside cut cavity of fish. Rub oil on both sides of fish, then wrap with bacon, leaving head and tail exposed. Heat grill. Set fish in center, then cover and cook 10–15 minutes, turning once, until opaque but still moist in thickest part. Remove from grill. Set bacon aside. Peel off top layer of skin. Slide fish onto serving platter. To serve, slide a wide spatula between flesh and bones, and lift out each portion. Serve with bacon on the side.

Editor's Extra: Fresh herbs could be tarragon, thyme, basil, or marjoram, or a combination.

Rotisserie Grilled Fish

1 (3- to 4-pound) whole fish, head and tail removed
½ stick butter
1 teaspoon parsley flakes
2 cloves garlic, minced
2 tablespoons lemon juice

Remove backbone, but do not cut fish in half. In a small saucepan over low heat, slowly melt butter with parsley flakes and garlic. Remove from heat, and add lemon juice. Sprinkle inside of fish with salt and pepper, if desired, then brush with butter mixture. Place in basket of rotisserie. Brush outside of fish with butter mixture. Cook in preheated rotisserie till flaky, about 20 minutes, brushing once or twice with butter mixture during cooking period.

Island Fish Fillets

⅓ cup teriyaki sauce
2 tablespoons lemon juice
1 pound fish fillets
¾ teaspoon Greek seasoning
¼ cup thinly sliced green onions and tops

Combine teriyaki sauce with lemon juice. Place fish in single layer in shallow baking pan; pour teriyaki mixture over fish and marinate 5 minutes on each side. Sprinkle fish with seasoning, then bake in sauce in preheated 350° oven 10–15 minutes, or until fish flake easily with fork. Place fish on serving platter, sprinkle with green onions, and spoon sauce over all. Serve immediately. Makes 4 servings.

The **five** largest lakes in the United States are the Great Lakes, located in the northeastern part of the United States along the Canadian border.

The Great Lakes are the largest group of fresh water lakes on Earth. They have a combined surface area of 95,000 square miles, and comprise about 25% of the world's freshwater reserves. Despite their size, large sections of the lakes freeze over in winter.

- Lake Superior is the largest by volume, and the deepest.
- Lake Michigan, the only one located entirely within U.S. borders, is the second largest by volume and third largest by area.
- Lake Huron is the third largest by volume; the second largest in area.
- Lake Erie is the smallest by volume, and the shallowest.
- Lake Ontario is the second smallest in volume, and the smallest in area.

Ranch Broiled Fish

1 envelope ranch dressing mix
⅓ cup lemon juice
3 tablespoons olive oil
3 tablespoons dry white wine or water
2 pounds red snapper or sole

Blend dressing mix, lemon juice, olive oil, and wine in a shallow dish. Add fish and coat well on both sides, then refrigerate, covered, 15–30 minutes.

Place on broiler pan, and broil 9–12 minutes or till fish flake easily when tested with a fork. Serves 4.

Potato Crusted Fish Fillets

2 eggs, beaten
½ cup fresh lemon juice
1 teaspoon Greek seasoning
1 (4-ounce) pouch roasted garlic mashed potatoes
6 white fish fillets, about ¾ inch thick

Preheat oven to 400°. Cover broiler pan with foil, then spray foil with nonstick cooking spray. In a shallow bowl, beat together eggs and lemon juice; add seasoning. Empty pouch of potatoes into separate shallow bowl. Dip fillets in egg mixture, then coat on both sides with dry potatoes. Place fillets on prepared pan, and bake in preheated oven 10–15 minutes. Set oven to broil, then broil 1–2 minutes, or till lightly browned. (Watch closely, or set your timer.) Serves 6.

Editor's Extra: Fillets may be grilled or sautéed in hot oil.

Fish Dressed for Dinner

1 pound frozen fish fillets
¼ cup Miracle Whip
2 tablespoons pesto
½ teaspoon salt
1 cup chopped tomato

Preheat oven to 450°. Place frozen fish in 9x13-inch baking dish. Combine dressing and pesto, and spread over fish. Sprinkle with salt and tomato. Bake about 15 minutes, or until fish flake easily when tested with a fork.

Fish and Chips the Easy Way

2 large baking potatoes, washed
¼ cup zesty Italian dressing
1 package fish fry coating mix, divided
1 pound white fish fillets, such as haddock,
**   halibut, or cod**
¼ cup mayonnaise-style salad dressing

Preheat oven to 400°. Cut each potato lengthwise into 8 wedges. Put Italian dressing in large bowl with potatoes, and toss to coat. Arrange cut sides down around outer edges of greased jellyroll pan. Bake 20 minutes.

Meanwhile, reserve ¼ cup coating mix, and set aside. Put remaining coating mix in shallow bowl. Spread each fish fillet on both sides with salad dressing, then coat with coating mix, pressing gently so coating will adhere.

Remove potatoes from oven; turn over. Place fish in center of baking sheet. Sprinkle reserved ¼ cup coating mix evenly over potatoes. Bake 15 minutes or until fish flake easily with fork.

Five-Minute Fish Amandine

2 tablespoons butter, divided
4 firm white fish fillets
¼ cup sliced almonds
1 teaspoon grated lemon zest
2 teaspoons fresh lemon juice

In a large skillet over medium-high heat, melt 1 table-spoon butter. Add fish. Cook 3–4 minutes per side, or until fish flake easily with a fork. Remove and keep warm.

Return skillet to stove over medium heat. Add remaining butter. Toast almonds, stirring frequently, until lightly brown. Add zest and juice, and cook 1 minute. Pour sauce over fish. Serves 4.

Buttery Lime-Basted Catfish

1 tablespoon butter
½ teaspoon garlic salt
2 tablespoons lime juice
½ teaspoon Creole seasoning
2 catfish fillets

Preheat broiler. Melt butter in a saucepan over medium heat. Stir in garlic salt, lime juice, and Creole seasoning. Remove from heat; set aside. In ungreased baking dish, generously brush fish with butter sauce. Broil 5–8 minutes, till fish flake easily with a fork. To serve, pour sauce over each fillet.

Crispy Catfish and Veggie Strips

1 pound fresh catfish fillets
4 cups crushed cornflakes
1 cup bottled ranch salad dressing
2 teaspoons bottled hot sauce
1 medium zucchini, halved, cut into strips

Rinse fish, and pat dry. Cut into 1-inch-wide strips. Put cornflakes in large zipper bag. Combine dressing and hot sauce in a shallow dish. Reserve half the sauce mixture for dipping. To remaining half, add catfish and zucchini strips, and stir to coat. Add ⅓ of zucchini and fish to the bag with cornflakes; seal, and shake to coat. Place coated zucchini and fish in a single layer on a greased 10x15-inch baking pan. Repeat with remaining zucchini and fish. Bake in 425° oven about 15 minutes or until fish flake easily with a fork. Serve with remaining sauce. Serves 4.

Crunchy Catfish Fillets

⅔ cup crushed cornflakes
½ teaspoon salt
¼ teaspoon cayenne pepper
4 (4-ounce) catfish fillets
2 egg whites, lightly beaten

Preheat oven to 450°. Mix together cornflakes, salt, and pepper in a shallow bowl. Rinse fillets; pat dry. Dip fillets in egg whites, then coat with crumb mixture. Place fillets in a baking pan lined with foil and sprayed with nonstick spray. Bake about 10 minutes, or until fish flake easily when tested with a fork. Serves 4.

There are **five** oceans in the world. All **five** oceans are connected.

- The Pacific Ocean is the largest and covers a third of the earth's surface.
- The Atlantic Ocean is second largest and occupies about 20% of the earth's surface. It is the most heavily traveled ocean.
- The Indian Ocean is third largest and covers approximately one-seventh of the earth's surface.
- The Antarctic Ocean surrounds the southern continent of Antarctica.
- The smallest of the earth's **five** ocean basins is the Arctic, which covers the earth's north pole. At lower latitudes, the ice melts during the summer months. At polar latitudes, however, the ice cover is permanent.

Beer-Battered Catfish

1 pound catfish fillets
1½ cups self-rising flour
⅓ cup fresh lemon juice
⅔ cup beer
¾ cup oil

Wash fish, and pat dry. Coat with flour; set aside. Combine remaining flour with lemon juice and beer, stirring until smooth. Heat oil in large skillet over medium-high heat. Meanwhile, dip fish in batter. Fry fish until golden brown on both sides. Serve with hushpuppies, coleslaw, and sweet tea.

Lemon-y Good Orange Roughy

1½ pounds orange roughy
1 teaspoon garlic powder
¼ cup butter, melted
¼ cup lemon juice
¼ cup soy sauce

Thaw fish, if frozen; rinse, and pat dry. Sprinkle fish with garlic powder. Combine butter, lemon juice, and soy sauce in a shallow dish. Marinate fish in butter mixture 15 minutes.

Place fillets in lightly greased broiler pan; broil 3–4 inches from heat for about 10 minutes, turning once. Fish are done when they flake easily with a fork. Garnish with paprika, if desired. Serves 4.

Parmesan Flounder Fillets

¼ cup Italian bread crumbs
½ teaspoon salt
¼ cup grated Parmesan cheese
1 pound flounder or sole fillets
¼ cup real mayonnaise

In shallow dish or on sheet of wax paper, combine crumbs, salt, and cheese. Brush all sides of fillets with mayonnaise; coat with crumb mixture. Arrange in single layer in shallow baking pan. Bake at 375° for 20–25 minutes, or until golden and fish flake easily. Serves 4.

A starfish has **five** pointy legs arranged like the points of a star. As these creatures are not actually fish, rather echinoderms, most marine biologists prefer to replace the term starfish with the less misleading term, sea star.

French Stuffed Flounder

½ cup French salad dressing, divided
1 pound flounder fillets
¾ cup crushed seasoned croutons
¼ cup finely chopped celery
½ teaspoon Cajun seasoning

Brush 2 tablespoons French salad dressing on top side of fillets. In small bowl, combine ¼ cup dressing, croutons, celery, and seasoning; equally divide mixture on fillets and roll up. Brush fillets with remaining 1 tablespoon dressing and bake at 350° for 35 minutes or until fish flake easily. Serves 4.

The Olympic Games have **five** interlocked rings as their symbol, representing the union of the **five** original continents (Africa, North and South America, Asia, Australia, and Europe), and the meeting of athletes from throughout the world at the Olympic Games. The colors of the rings are blue, yellow, black, green, and red. However, no continent is represented by any specific ring.

Zesty Baked Halibut

2 plum tomatoes, sliced ¼ inch thick
4 (4-ounce) halibut steaks
⅔ cup chopped onion
⅓ cup zesty Italian dressing
1½ tablespoons capers

Arrange ½ the tomato slices in the bottom of a 2-quart baking dish. Top with fish, onion, and remaining tomatoes. Drizzle with Italian dressing, then sprinkle with capers. Bake at 350° for 20–25 minutes or until fish flake easily with a fork.

Easy Halibut Bake

4 (6-ounce) halibut fillets
5 tablespoons olive oil, divided
2 medium tomatoes, sliced
2 cloves garlic
1 (6-ounce) can pitted ripe olives

Preheat oven to 375°. Arrange fillets in a baking pan. Brush with a tablespoon of oil. Place tomato slices over fish. Bake about 20 minutes, or until done.

Place garlic and olives in blender and blend until finely minced. Add remaining 4 tablespoons oil in a thin steady stream, and blend to form a paste. Spoon evenly over each fillet.

Grilled Tilapia Packets

4 (4-ounce) tilapia fillets
1 cup shredded carrots
1 cup sliced mushrooms
2 stalks celery, cut into ½-inch-thick slices
½ cup seafood marinade

Marinate fillets, carrots, mushrooms, and celery in seafood marinade 30 minutes in refrigerator, turning several times to coat evenly.

Cut 4 large sheets of heavy-duty foil. Place equal portions of fish and vegetables onto center of foil sheets. Loosely fold top and ends to seal each packet. Preheat grill over medium-high heat. Grill about 10 minutes, or until fish flake easily with a fork. Poke foil with knife to release steam before opening the packets. Can eat directly from packet, or serve on plates with juice poured over.

Breaded Baked Tilapia

4 tilapia fillets
2 tablespoons lemon juice
1½ cups white wine
½ cup butter, melted, divided
1 cup fine bread crumbs

Place fillets on baking pan, and drizzle with lemon juice, wine, and ½ the butter. Sprinkle with salt and pepper to taste. Bake at 350° for 20 minutes, or until fish flake easily with a fork; remove from oven.

Turn heat to broil. Sprinkle fish with bread crumbs, and drizzle with remaining ¼ cup butter. Broil for just a few minutes, watching closely so it doesn't burn, until fish is lightly browned. Serves 4.

Snappy Red Snapper

4 small red snapper fillets
1/2 cup chili sauce
1 cup seeded and chopped tomato
2 small yellow crookneck squash, sliced
1/4 cup grated Parmesan cheese

Wash fillets, and pat dry. Place red snapper in glass baking dish, with thickest parts to outside. Cover with plastic wrap, venting one corner. Microwave on HIGH 3 minutes. Drain. Spread 2 tablespoons chili sauce over each fillet, and place tomato and squash slices over sauce. Sprinkle with cheese. Cover again with more plastic wrap. Microwave on HIGH 3–4 minutes, or until fish flake easily when tested with a fork. Serves 4.

Italian Salmon

1 envelope dry Italian salad dressing mix
1/2 cup water
2 tablespoons lemon juice
6 (4-ounce) salmon fillets
1 cup fresh sliced mushrooms

Preheat oven to 350°. Combine salad dressing mix, water, and lemon juice. Place salmon in a single layer in a lightly greased 9x13-inch baking dish. Pour dressing mixture over top, then sprinkle with sliced mushrooms. Cover with foil, and bake 15 minutes. Remove foil, baste with dressing mixture, and bake 15 minutes more. Serves 6.

Grilled Salmon with Cilantro Cream

2 tablespoons Greek vinaigrette dressing, divided
¼ cup sour cream
3 tablespoons finely chopped fresh cilantro
1 small clove garlic, minced
2 (4-ounce) salmon fillets

Combine 1 tablespoon dressing, sour cream, cilantro, and garlic in a small bowl until well blended; chill until ready to serve.

Place remaining tablespoon dressing in a shallow bowl. Add salmon, skin side up, in dressing to coat. Grill salmon skin side down over medium heat for 10 minutes, or until fish flake easily with a fork. To serve, top with cilantro cream mixture.

Salmon Steaks Made Easy

4 (4-ounce) salmon fillets
2 tablespoons orange juice
¼ cup soy sauce
1 clove garlic, minced
1 tablespoon butter

Wash salmon fillets and pat dry. In a small saucepan, combine orange juice, soy sauce, garlic, and butter over medium-high heat. Cook until mixtures thickens enough to coat back of spoon. Coat both sides of salmon with soy sauce mixture. Marinate in refrigerator 1–2 hours.

Preheat oven to 450°. Bake in a lightly greased 2-quart baking dish 10–15 minutes, or until fish flake easily when tested with a fork. Serves 4.

Breaded Salmon Dijon

4 (6-ounce) salmon fillets
2½ tablespoons Dijon mustard
¼ cup dry Italian bread crumbs
¼ cup butter, melted
½ teaspoon lemon pepper

Preheat oven to 400°. Wash salmon fillets and pat dry. Line a jellyroll pan with foil. Place fillets on foil, skin side down. Spread top and sides of each fillet with about 2 teaspoons mustard. Top mustard with a layer of bread crumbs and sprinkle with lemon pepper. Add salt to taste. Drizzle butter over top. Bake about 15 minutes, or until fish flake easily when tested with a fork. May add a little pepper, if desired. Serves 4.

Simple Salmon Croquettes

Quick and easy, and the kids love 'em!

1 (14¾-ounce) can salmon, undrained
1 egg
1 cup self-rising flour
1 teaspoon onion powder
⅓ cup oil

Remove bones and skin from salmon. In medium bowl, combine salmon and egg. Stir in flour and onion powder. Heat oil in large skillet over medium-high heat. Drop salmon mixture by ¼ cupfuls into hot oil, flatten slightly, and fry on both sides until golden brown. Remove from oil, and sprinkle with salt to taste.

Tomato Salmon Stacks

Pretty, tasty, and easy.

2 large tomatoes, sliced into 4 rounds each
½ teaspoon salt
1 (16-ounce) can salmon, drained, flaked
1 tablespoon lemon juice
4 slices American cheese

Preheat broiler. Place 4 tomato slices on a baking sheet covered with foil. Evenly divide salmon among each tomato slice. Sprinkle salmon with lemon juice, then top with another slice of tomato. Season to taste with salt and pepper. Top with cheese. Broil 6 inches from heat, about 5 minutes or until cheese melts. May add extra salt and a little pepper, if desired. Serves 4.

Editor's Extra: Tuna or chicken are also superb, either canned, vacuum-packed, or freshly cooked. And great to sub Swiss, Cheddar, Muenster, or Colby cheese.

Tuna Alfredo

3 cups mini lasagna noodles
½ cup basil pesto
1 (10-ounce) container refrigerated Alfredo sauce
1 (12-ounce) can solid white tuna, drained, flaked
⅓ cup grated Parmesan cheese

Cook pasta according to directions; drain. Preheat oven to 400°. Combine pesto and Alfredo sauce. Add along with tuna to cooked pasta; stir to combine. Transfer to a lightly greased 2-quart casserole dish. Sprinkle with Parmesan. Bake about 20 minutes, until cheese melts. Serves 6.

Quinary (**base-5**) is a numeral system with **five** as the base. This originates from the **five** fingers on either hand, the most primitive numeral system.

Roman numerals use the **quinary** as the sub-base. **Five** is written as V, **50** is L, **500** is D, but **25** (square of **5**) is written as XXV, **125** (cube of **5**) is written as CXXV. This is superimposed on a decimal base, which is sometimes referred to as the **quinary**-decimal system.

In the 20th century, only the East African Luo tribe of Kenya and the Yoruba of Nigeria were still using a **base-five** system. The base-ten (denary or decimal) system has prevailed in most areas, and almost all of the previously **quinary**-counting cultures have converted.

Golden Fried Shrimp

You'll be slapping hands the whole time you're frying these (to keep everyone out of them!).

4 pounds large shrimp, peeled, deveined
1½ teaspoons Cajun seasoning
1 teaspoon ground black pepper
8 eggs, beaten
1½ cups all-purpose flour

Season shrimp with Cajun seasoning and pepper in a large bowl; stir to coat well. In a medium bowl, blend eggs with flour. Coat shrimp with egg batter, then deep-fry in hot oil (don't crowd them) till golden brown.

Buttery Shrimp Scampi

½ cup butter
5 cloves garlic, minced
2 tablespoons lemon juice
2 tablespoons chopped fresh parsley
1 pound medium shrimp, peeled, deveined

Place butter, garlic, lemon juice, and parsley in a medium skillet. Cook uncovered over medium-high heat about 4 minutes, or until butter is melted. Add shrimp; stir to coat well. May season with Cajun seasoning to taste, if desired. Cook until shrimp turn pink and curl slightly. Don't overcook. Remove from heat and let sit a few minutes before serving.

According to one survey, Americans use **five** times the amount of water that Europeans use. Can you believe that during a **five**-minute shower, we use twenty-**five** to **fifty** gallons of water!

Hot Soppin' Shrimp

Get out the paper towels and enjoy this messy but fantastic shrimp dish.

1 stick butter
4 pounds shrimp, unpeeled
Juice of 1 lemon
1 (8-ounce) bottle Italian dressing
1/2–1 teaspoon cracked black pepper

Melt butter in large roasting pan. Put shrimp, lemon juice, and dressing in pan. Sprinkle with black pepper. Cover tightly and bake at 350° about 45 minutes. Peel as you eat. Have French bread available for sopping up the tasty sauce.

Shrimp Linguine

6 ounces spinach linguine
3 tablespoons butter
1½ pounds medium shrimp, peeled, deveined
2 teaspoons chopped fresh basil,
**   or 1 teaspoon dried basil**
½ teaspoon salt

Prepare linguine according to package directions; drain. Keep warm. Melt butter in large skillet over medium-high heat; add shrimp and basil, and cook for a few minutes, till shrimp turn pink and curl, stirring frequently. Sprinkle with salt. Serve shrimp and sauce over warm linguine. Serves 4.

Shrimp Quesadillas

4 large flour tortillas, divided
2 cups shredded Monterey Jack Cheese with
  jalapeños, divided
1 (12-ounce) bag frozen salad shrimp, rinsed, drained
1 cup sour cream
1 cup frozen seasoning blend, thawed

Place 2 tortillas on lightly oiled flat baking pan. Sprinkle with half the cheese. Top cheese with shrimp. Mix sour cream with seasoning blend, and spread over shrimp. Top with remaining cheese. Place remaining tortillas on top, and brush lightly with oil. Bake at 375° for 10–15 minutes, or until cheese melts and tortilla surface is slightly crispy. Serve with salsa.

Editor's Extra: If you can't find frozen seasoning blend in the frozen vegetable section of your grocery store, you can make up your own mix of chopped onions, bell peppers, celery, and parsley.

Scrumptious Skewered Shrimp

1 (8-ounce) bottle Italian dressing
1 cup chili sauce
2 tablespoons corn syrup
2 pounds large shrimp, peeled, deveined
4 lemons, cut into wedges

In large bowl, blend Italian dressing with chili sauce and corn syrup; add shrimp. Cover and marinate in refrigerator 2 hours, turning occasionally. On skewers, alternately thread shrimp and lemons. Grill about 10 minutes or until done, turning and basting frequently with remaining marinade. Serves 6.

Grilled Spicy Skewered Shrimp

20 jumbo raw shrimp in tails, peeled, deveined
1 tablespoon vegetable oil
1 teaspoon lemon juice
1 clove garlic, minced
1 tablespoon five-spice powder

Skewer 4 shrimp on 5 skewers, or 5 shrimp on 4 skewers, or if they are really big, 3 may be enough. Mix remaining ingredients in shallow bowl. Rub each shrimp with mixture. Grill 2 minutes on each side on hot grill. Serves 4–5.

Editor's Extra: Good with grilled vegetables, grilled buttered hoagie bread halves, and cole slaw or potato salad.

Cajun Shrimp Boil

1 pound Cajun sausage
1 (6-ounce) package dry crab boil
6 cups water
6 ears fresh corn, broken in half
3 pounds medium shrimp, peeled, deveined

Slice sausage into ½-inch pieces. Place crab boil and sausage in water and boil 30 minutes. Add corn; cook 6 minutes. (May need to add more water during cook time to make sure ingredients are completely covered.) Add shrimp; season with salt and pepper to taste; boil 3 minutes, stirring occasionally. Drain. Serves 8.

Homemade Cocktail Sauce

1 cup ketchup
1 tablespoon lemon juice
4 tablespoons horseradish
1 teaspoon Worcestershire
¼ teaspoon onion powder

Mix all ingredients well; add a little Tabasco, if desired. Store in jar in refrigerator.

Five-spice powder is a convenient seasoning for Chinese cuisine that incorporates the **five** basic flavors of Chinese cooking—sweet, sour, bitter, pungent, and salty. It typically consists of equal parts cinnamon, cloves, fennel seed, star anise, and Szechuan pepper.

Worcesterbutter Sauce

½ cup butter or margarine
1 tablespoon chopped parsley
2 tablespoons lemon juice
1½ teaspoons Worcestershire
¼ teaspoon black pepper

Melt butter in a small saucepan. Stir in remaining ingredients. Heat thoroughly. Serve over fish or vegetables.

Quick and Easy Tartar Sauce

2 cups mayonnaise
3 tablespoons sweet pickle relish
2 tablespoons hot sauce
1 teaspoon lemon juice
1 teaspoon paprika

Stir together mayonnaise, relish, hot sauce, lemon juice, and paprika. Keep refrigerated till serving time.

Fast
and
Fabulous

FIVE ★ STAR

Cakes

"**Hang Five**" is a term used in surfing, in which a surfer will stand at the front of a surf board and wrap the **five** toes of one foot around the front of the surfboard. To "hang ten" is to wrap the ten toes of the feet around the front of the surfboard.

Although the origins of surfing are obscure, it is clear that it developed in Hawaii, where it was popular during the 19th century. It spread to the California coast during the 1920s and became very popular with American youth in the 1960s. With lifestyles freer than those of most athletes, surfers comprise a unique sporting sub-cult. Though surfing is practiced in many other Pacific nations, its mecca remains Hawaii, where the international surfing championships are held annually.

Proud-To-Take Pound Cake

1 (18¼-ounce) box butter cake mix
½ stick butter, softened
¼ cup vegetable oil
1 (8-ounce) carton sour cream
3 large eggs

Preheat oven to 350°. Mix all ingredients together well—at least 5 minutes. Bake in greased and floured tube or Bundt pan 50 minutes.

Editor's Extra: I was making this one time and the batter was too thick (maybe my eggs were too small), so I added 2 tablespoons buttermilk—it was perfect! It often pays to be creative.

Big-On-Vanilla Butter Pound Cake

3 sticks butter, softened
3½ cups confectioners' sugar
6 eggs
3½ cups sifted cake flour
1 tablespoon vanilla extract

Preheat oven to 325°. Cream butter and sugar until light and fluffy. Add eggs one at a time, beating well after each addition. Gradually add flour. Add vanilla and beat well. Pour batter into a greased 10-inch tube pan. Bake for 45 minutes or until cake tests done.

A Touch of Orange Pound Cake

2 sticks real butter, softened
2 cups sugar
3 eggs
2 cups self-rising flour
2 tablespoons orange juice

Preheat oven to 350°. Cream butter with sugar till fluffy. Add eggs one at a time, beating well after each addition. Gradually mix in flour and orange juice. Pour into well-greased and floured Bundt or tube pan. Bake 1 hour, or until cake tests done.

The Real Deal Pound Cake

1 pound butter, softened
3½ cups sugar
8 eggs, separated
1 teaspoon lemon extract
4½ cups sifted all-purpose flour (measure
   after sifting)

Preheat oven to 325°. In large mixer bowl, beat butter and sugar until light and fluffy. Add egg yolks one at a time, beating well after each addition. Add lemon extract. Gradually add flour, beating well after each addition. Beat egg whites till stiff, then fold into flour mixture. Pour batter into well-greased tube pan, and bake 90 minutes or until cake tests done.

Hint of Lemon Pound Cake

2 cups sugar
1 cup butter-flavored shortening
6 eggs
2 cups self-rising flour
2 teaspoons lemon extract

Cream sugar and shortening. Beat in eggs, one at a time. Gradually add flour. Stir in lemon extract. Pour batter into greased and floured tube pan, and bake at 350° for 1 hour.

Blueberry Pound Cake

1 (18¼-ounce) box butter cake mix
1 (8-ounce) carton cream cheese, softened
½ cup oil
3 eggs, beaten
1 (15-ounce) can whole blueberries

Beat cake mix, cream cheese, oil, and eggs with electric mixer until smooth. Add blueberries, and stir by hand until mixed. Bake in greased and floured Bundt pan at 350° for 1 hour.

Chocolate Coconut Pound Cake

1 frozen pound cake, thawed
1 (7-ounce) package flaked coconut
1 (14-ounce) can sweetened condensed milk
½ cup chopped toasted almonds
1 (16-ounce) can fudge frosting

Slice cake horizontally into 4 layers. Stir together coconut and condensed milk till well blended. Spoon half the coconut mixture on one layer. Sprinkle half the almonds over the coconut mixture. Place another cake layer on top, and spread with fudge frosting. Repeat layers, ending with frosting.

5

Lite Angelic Chocolate Cake

1 ready-made angel food cake
1 cup skim milk
1 (3-ounce) package milk chocolate instant pudding
2 cups frozen low-fat whipped topping, thawed
1 (1.4-ounce) Heath bar, chopped

Split cake horizontally with long serrated knife to make 2 layers. Beat milk and pudding mix in large bowl until well blended. Fold in whipped topping. Spread ½ of chocolate mixture between cake layers. Top with remaining mixture. Refrigerate 1 hour before serving. Sprinkle top with chopped candy bar. Store leftover cake in refrigerator.

Almond Chocolate Cream Angel Cake

6 tablespoons cocoa
6 tablespoons sugar
3 cups whipping cream
1 cup sliced almonds, toasted, divided
1 large angel food cake

Mix cocoa and sugar with cream; chill 1 hour. Whip cream mixture until stiff peaks form, then add ½ cup almonds.

Cut a 1-inch slice from top of cake. Carefully cut a trench inside cake, leaving walls and bottom approximately 1-inch thick. Fill cake with ⅓ of cocoa cream. Place top on cake and frost with remaining cocoa cream. Sprinkle with remaining almonds. Chill well before serving.

Take 5 is a Hershey's candy bar combining **five** flavors: milk chocolate, pretzel, caramel, peanut, and peanut butter. Due to its popularity, the Hershey's Company has produced several variations of the original bar:

- White Chocolate–has a white chocolate coating instead of milk chocolate.
- Peanut Butter–has a peanut butter coating instead of milk chocolate.
- Chocolate Cookie–substitutes a chocolate cookie to replace the pretzel.
- Marshmallow–substitutes a marshmallow crème to replace the caramel.

Take 5 ice cream bars have a combination of **five** ingredients: peanut butter ice cream, peanuts, caramel, pretzels, and milk chocolate coating. In spring of 2006, McDonald's began offering **Take 5** in their McFlurry treats.

Holly's Snowball Surprise

All of Holly's favorites are in this cake!

1 large angel food cake, white or chocolate
1 (16-ounce) container frozen Cool Whip, thawed,
**   divided**
2 tablespoons green crème de menthe liqueur
2 (2.5-ounce) packages chocolate instant mousse
1⅓ cups cold milk

With a long sharp knife, cut top ¼ of angel food cake off horizontally. Then cut a trench around entire cake, leaving enough margin on sides to hold cake up. Remove small pieces of cake from trench, leaving it 3 inches deep and 2 inches wide. Cut pieces of cake small, then mix with ½ cup Cool Whip and crème de menthe in a small bowl. Set aside.

Mix chocolate mousse mix and cold milk in medium bowl 2–3 minutes, till thick. Place cake on serving plate and fill trench with chocolate mousse. Fill center hole of cake with crème de menthe mixture. Replace cake top, and frost entire cake with remaining Cool Whip. Voilà! A snowball! Refrigerate to set.

Editor's Extra: Fun to decorate with chocolate sprinkles or green or red cherry halves around the base.

Ambrosia Cake

1 (10-inch) sponge or angel food cake
2 cups sour cream
1 (20-ounce) can crushed pineapple, drained
¼ cup light brown sugar, packed
1 (11-ounce) can Mandarin orange sections, drained

Evenly cut cake into 3 horizontal layers. Stir together sour cream, crushed pineapple, and brown sugar. Place a layer of cake on serving platter. Top with ⅓ of pineapple mixture. Repeat 2 more times. Arrange Mandarin orange sections over top; chill well. Must be kept refrigerated.

Sweet Bottoms

This is great for strawberry shortcake, or as a base for any kind of juicy fruits. Add a dollop of whipped cream on top.

2 cups self-rising flour
½ cup sugar
½ cup butter or butter-flavored shortening
2 eggs, beaten
⅔ cup evaporated milk

Mix flour and sugar; cut in butter until mix is like coarse crumbs. Add eggs and milk; stir only to moisten. Bake in 12 greased tart pans or an 8-inch cake pan at 350° for 15–20 minutes. Freezes well.

Superb Strawberry Shortcake

5¼ cups baking mix
6 tablespoons sugar
1¼ cups milk
6 tablespoons butter, melted
2 (10-ounce) packages frozen, sweetened
   strawberries, thawed

Preheat oven to 425°. In a large mixing bowl, mix baking mix, sugar, milk, and butter. Roll out dough on lightly floured board to ½-inch thickness. Cut into 4-inch rounds. Bake at 425° for 8–10 minutes. Serve with strawberries and juice on top. Top with whipped cream, if desired.

The Supreme Court of the United States is the highest court in the United States, having ultimate judicial authority to interpret and decide questions of federal law.

The court consists of nine justices: the chief justice of the United States and eight associate justices of the Supreme Court of the United States. The justices are nominated by the president and confirmed with the "advice and consent" of the senate. Appointed to serve for life, they can be removed only by retirement, resignation, or impeachment and subsequent conviction.

Five is the number necessary to make a majority decision in the U.S. Supreme Court. Several years ago, the Supreme Court delivered a highly controversial **5**–4 decision in Bush v. Gore (2000), that ended weeks of bitter legal maneuvering between lower courts following the 2000 presidential election.

Heavenly Pineapple Whipped Cream Cake

1 (8¼-ounce) can crushed pineapple, drained
½ pint whipping cream, whipped
1 (3-ounce) package vanilla instant pudding
1 cup milk
1 prepared angel food cake

Combine pineapple and whipped cream. Prepare pudding, using only 1 cup milk. Add to pineapple mixture. Slice cake into 3 horizontal layers. Spread pineapple filling between layers; frost top and sides of cake. Chill before serving.

Creamy Pineapple Cake

1 purchased angel food cake
1 (8-ounce) tub whipped cream cheese
6 ounces pineapple preserves
1 (16-ounce) container extra creamy whipped topping
1 fresh pineapple, cored, sliced into rings

Slice angel food cake in half horizontally. Set top half of cake aside. In a small bowl, mix cream cheese and preserves, adding more or less preserves to taste. Spread all of cream cheese mixture thickly on bottom half of angel food cake. Place top half of cake on top of cream cheese mixture, fitting both cake halves together. Frost entire cake with extra creamy whipped topping (or real whipped cream, if you like!). Place pineapple rings in a pattern on top of and around sides of cake.

Fabulous Frosted Angel Cake

1 purchased angel food cake
3 cups heavy cream
1 cup brown sugar
1 (20-ounce) can crushed pineapple, drained
⅔ cup finely chopped pecans

Slice cake into 3 horizontal layers. In mixing bowl, stir together cream and brown sugar, and beat till stiff peaks form. Gently stir in pineapple and pecans. Spread frosting between layers and on top and sides. Chill well before serving.

Pineapple Cherry Cake

1 (20-ounce) can cherry pie filling
1 (18¼-ounce) box yellow cake mix
1 (20-ounce) can crushed pineapple, drained
2 sticks butter, softened
1–1½ cups chopped pecans

Preheat oven to 350°. Grease a 9x13-inch casserole dish. In large bowl, combine pie filling, cake mix, pineapple, butter, and pecans, and blend well. Pour into prepared dish, and bake about 1 hour, or until cake springs back when lightly touched.

Editor's Extra: If desired, you can substitute apple pie filling for the cherry.

The spinal column in mammals, as in other vertebrates, is composed of a series of small bones. In many mammals the vertebrae can be seen to be divided into **five** distinct regions (though in some groups such as the whales, they are pretty indistinct).

- Cervical Vertebrae– the neck region.
- Thoracic Vertebrae– the rib bones extend from here.
- Lumbar Vertebrae– the third section down to where the back legs connect.
- Sacral Vertebrae– support the pelvic girdle and are often fused together.
- Caudal Vertebrae– the bones of the tail. They also do not contain the spinal column, which ends at or before the sacral vertebrae (known as the coccyx in humans).

Mammals, including humans, have **five** parts to their fore limbs (or arms):

- Upper arm (humerus)
- Forearm (ulna plus radius)
- Wrist (carpel bones)
- Palm of Hand (metacarpel bones)
- Fingers (phalanges or digits)

Sour Cream Apple Cake

1 stick butter, melted
3 eggs, divided
1 (18¼-ounce) box butter-flavored cake mix
1 (20-ounce) can apple pie filling
1 (16-ounce) carton sour cream

Preheat oven to 350°. In large mixing bowl, combine butter, 2 eggs, and dry cake mix, and blend well. Pour into greased 9x13-inch baking pan. Bake for 25 minutes. Spoon pie filling over cake.

In small bowl, combine sour cream and remaining egg. Pour mixture over pie filling. Continue baking 15 minutes, or until sour cream topping is set.

Luscious Lemon Cake

1 (18¼-ounce) package lemon cake mix
3 eggs
1 cup plus 3 tablespoons sour cream, divided
1 (3-ounce) package cream cheese, softened
⅓ cup oil

Preheat oven to 350°. In mixer bowl, blend cake mix, eggs, 1 cup sour cream, cream cheese, and oil until moistened. Beat 2 minutes on medium speed. Pour into greased 9x13-inch baking pan. Bake for 30–40 minutes or until toothpick inserted in center comes out clean. Cool cake in pan on cooling rack. Refrigerate leftovers.

Editor's Extra: Even nicer with a glaze of 2 tablespoons lemon juice mixed with 1¼ cups confectioners' sugar.

Jean's Supreme Cake

1 (18¼-ounce) box lemon supreme cake mix
3 eggs
1 stick butter, softened
½ (8-ounce) carton frozen whipped topping, thawed
½ cup oil

Preheat oven to 350°. In large mixer bowl, beat ingredients until smooth. Bake in greased and floured Bundt pan for 45 minutes.

Editor's Extra: Try orange or pineapple, yellow, or chocolate cake mix—any kind is good.

Old Favorite Lemon Jell-O Cake

1 (18¼-ounce) box lemon or yellow cake mix
1 (3-ounce) box lemon Jell-O
4 eggs
1 cup milk
¾ cup vegetable oil

Mix together cake mix, Jell-O, eggs, and milk. Add oil and mix well. Bake in a greased tube pan at 350° for 55 minutes or until tests done. Can also be baked in a greased 9x13-inch pan for 30 minutes.

Editor's Extra: Glaze with ⅓ cup sugared lemon juice, if desired.

Apricot Nectar Cake

1 (18¼-ounce) box lemon cake mix
1 (12-ounce) can apricot nectar
¾ cup vegetable oil
4 eggs
½ cup sugar

Combine ingredients in order given. Bake in greased and floured tube pan at 325° for 1 hour.

Spice Pumpkin Cupcakes

1 (16-ounce) can solid-pack pumpkin
3 eggs
⅓ cup oil
⅓ cup water
1 (18¼-ounce) box spice cake mix

Preheat oven to 350°. In large mixing bowl, beat pumpkin, eggs, oil, and water till blended well. Add cake mix, and blend 2 more minutes. Fill 24 paper-lined muffin tins ¾ full. Bake about 18 minutes, or until toothpick inserted in center comes out clean.

Editor's Extra: Great all by itself, or frost with a can of cream cheese frosting, if desired.

Moist and Delicious Chess Cake

1 (18¼-ounce) box yellow cake mix
1 stick margarine, melted
3 eggs, divided
1 (8-ounce) package cream cheese, softened
2½ cups powdered sugar

Preheat oven to 325°. Stir cake mix, margarine, and 1 egg together well, and press into a lightly greased 9x13-inch pan. Beat cream cheese, powdered sugar, and remaining eggs together well, and pour over crust mixture. Bake 40 minutes. Do not open oven while baking!

Butter Pecan Coconut Cake

1 cup chopped pecans
1 (18¼-ounce) box butter pecan cake mix
4 eggs
⅔ cup vegetable oil
1 (15-ounce) can pecan coconut frosting

Preheat oven to 325°. Spread chopped nuts in bottom of Bundt pan that has been greased with shortening. In large bowl, mix cake mix, eggs, oil, and pecan coconut frosting. Pour batter over nuts. Bake 60 minutes or until cake tests done.

Funny Cake

2 eggs
1 (18¼-ounce) white or yellow cake mix
1 cup brown sugar
1 cup miniature marshmallows
1 cup chocolate chips

Preheat oven to 350°. Break eggs into a measuring cup and beat with a whisk. Add water to make ⅔ cup. In mixer, beat cake mix, brown sugar, and eggs, and place in a greased 9x13-inch cake pan. Sprinkle with marshmallows and chocolate chips. Bake for 25–30 minutes. Cool.

James Monroe, fifth president of the United States

James Monroe (1758–1831) was the **fifth** president of the United States and served two terms in office (1817–1825). In both elections, Monroe ran nearly uncontested.

His administration was marked by the acquisition of Florida (1819); the Missouri Compromise (1820), an agreement passed between the proslavery and antislavery factions in the United States involving primarily the regulation of slavery in the western territories; and the Monroe Doctrine (1823), declaring U.S. opposition to European interference in the Americas.

Five states entered the Union while Monroe was in office:

- Mississippi (1817)
- Illinois (1818)
- Alabama (1818)
- Maine (1820)
- Missouri (1821)

Éclair Cake

Always a favorite, and so easy to prepare.

2 (3-ounce) boxes French vanilla instant pudding
3 cups cold milk
1 (8-ounce) tub frozen whipped topping, thawed
1 box graham crackers
1 (16-ounce) can chocolate frosting

Beat pudding mix and milk in large bowl until well blended. Fold in whipped topping. Put a layer of graham crackers in bottom of lightly greased 9x13-inch dish. Spread with ⅓ pudding mixture. Repeat 2 more times. Top with a layer of graham crackers. Refrigerate about 30 minutes. Spread top with frosting.

Mini Orange Cheesecakes

5 navel oranges
½ cup granola cereal or graham crumbs
1 (8-ounce) package cream cheese, softened
1 (8-ounce) container vanilla yogurt
1 (8-ounce) container frozen whipped topping, thawed

Slice 1 inch from top end of each orange. Remove "lid" and set aside. With a tablespoon, scoop out orange close to the skin. Gently pull fruit from peel and reserve. Take a thin slice off bottom so orange will stand.

Place a tablespoonful of granola or crumbs in each orange shell, reserving some for tops. Separate reserved pulp from membrane and seeds with your hands. Measure 1 cup of pulp; discard membrane and seeds.

In mixer, beat the cream cheese until smooth. Blend in yogurt and pulp. Fold in whipped topping. Spoon into orange shells; refrigerate 4–5 hours to set. Sprinkle tops with reserved granola or crumbs. Fun to stick a birthday candle in each one.

White Chocolate Pudding Cheesecake

1 (8-ounce) package cream cheese, softened
1¼ cups cold milk, divided
1 (3½-ounce) package white chocolate instant
   pudding
1½ cups thawed Cool Whip
1 graham cracker pie crust

In large bowl, whisk cream cheese and ¼ cup milk till well blended. Beat in remaining 1 cup milk and pudding mix. Gently stir in Cool Whip till well blended; spoon into crust. Chill 4 hours or until set.

Editor's Extra: This is pretty garnished with chocolate curls or sprinkles.

Mini Cheesecakes
Kids like to make—and eat—these!

12 vanilla wafers
2 (8-ounce) packages cream cheese
½ cup sugar
1 teaspoon vanilla
2 eggs

Preheat oven to 325°. Place paper or foil liners in a 12-cup muffin pan. Put a vanilla wafer in each. Blend together cream cheese, sugar, and vanilla on medium speed. Add eggs, and mix well. Pour over wafers, filling ¾ full. Bake for 25 minutes. Allow to cool, then remove from pan. May top with fruit and nuts, if desired.

Editor's Extra: For an extra special treat, melt ½ cup chocolate chips in microwave for 1¾ minutes on HIGH, then drizzle over baked cheesecake.

The term concerto refers to a musical work in which one solo instrument is accompanied by an orchestra.

The number of completed, numbered piano concertos of German composer Ludwig van Beethoven (1770–1827) and French composer Camille Saint-Saëns (1835–1921) is **five**. Saint-Saëns also wrote **five** symphonies, although only three of these are numbered.

By the time German composer Felix Mendelssohn (1809–1847) was fourteen, he had written **five** concertos and twelve symphonies.

Austrian composer Wolfgang Amadeus Mozart (1756–1791) wrote "only" **five** violin concertos—all of them in the brief period from April to December 1775 while he was employed as a violinist in the court orchestra of Salzburg. However, in subsequent years Mozart made a reputation for himself chiefly as a pianist.

Impressive Chocolate Cheesecake Flan

1½ cups sugar, divided
6 semisweet chocolate baking squares, divided
1 (12-ounce) can evaporated milk
1 (8-ounce) package cream cheese, cubed
4 eggs

Preheat oven to 350°. In a small heavy saucepan, cook 1 cup sugar on medium heat until deep golden brown, stirring constantly. Pour into a greased 9-inch round cake pan. Microwave chocolate squares in a 4-cup glass measure on HIGH 1½ minutes or until chocolate is almost melted; cool. Blend milk and cream cheese in blender until smooth. Add remaining ½ cup sugar, eggs, and melted chocolate; cover and blend well. Pour over syrup in cake pan. Place pan in larger baking pan with enough water to come halfway up side of cake pan. Bake 1 hour or until knife inserted 1-inch from edge comes out clean. Cool on wire rack. Refrigerate 4 hours or overnight.

To unmold, run a knife around the edge, and invert onto a serving plate. Melt remaining 2 chocolate squares in glass measure on HIGH 1 minute or until melted. Drizzle chocolate with a spoon in 5 or 6 random crisscross designs onto a sheet of wax paper; let stand until firm. Carefully remove chocolate designs and place on top of flan to decorate.

Oreo Chip Muffin Cheesecakes

24 Oreo cookies
3 (8-ounce) packages cream cheese, softened
¾ cup sugar
3 eggs
½ cup chocolate chips

Preheat oven to 350°. Place Oreos in paper liners in 24 muffin tins. Beat together cream cheese, sugar, and eggs, adding one at a time. Spoon some cream cheese mixture over each cookie. Bake for 15–20 minutes or until center is almost set. Melt chocolate chips and drizzle each cheesecake with chocolate.

Fresh Raspberry Refrigerator Cake

2 pints fresh raspberries
2 cups (1 pint) heavy cream
½ cup sugar
1 teaspoon vanilla
3 (3-ounce) packages lady fingers, divided

Rinse raspberries lightly; drain. Save a few for a garnish. Beat cream with sugar and vanilla till stiff. Fill an 8-inch springform pan alternately with layers of lady fingers, raspberries, and whipped cream, using only 2 packages of lady fingers, ending with cream. . Chill 10–12 hours. Just before serving, remove sides from pan and place cake on serving plate. Stand remaining lady fingers around sides of cake, pressing lightly to adhere. Garnish with reserved raspberries. Serves 10.

Buttercream Frosting

⅔ cup milk
4 egg yolks
⅔ cup sugar
2 sticks butter, softened
2 teaspoons vanilla

In medium saucepan, bring milk to a boil. Meanwhile, beat egg yolks and sugar in medium bowl. Add a little hot milk to egg mixture to temper the eggs, then gradually add remaining milk. Return mixture to saucepan over medium-high heat, and cook until slightly thickened, stirring constantly. When thickened, strain mixture into a large bowl; allow to cool. Cream butter until fluffy, then gradually add cooled milk mixture, and stir until smooth. Stir in vanilla.

White Chocolate Frosting

1 (6-ounce) bag white chocolate chips
2 (8-ounce) packages cream cheese, softened
½ stick butter, softened
2 teaspoons vanilla
2½ cups confectioners' sugar

Melt white chocolate in microwave, then cool to lukewarm. Beat cream cheese and butter until fluffy. Add white chocolate and vanilla, then add sugar a little at a time, beating until smooth and of spreading consistency. Chill until ready to frost cake.

Classic Seven-Minute Frosting

2 large egg whites
1 cup sugar
¼ cup water
1 teaspoon white corn syrup
¼ teaspoon cream of tartar

In a double boiler over simmering water, beat egg whites with electric mixer until frothy; add remaining ingredients, and continue to beat until soft peaks form, about 7 minutes. Remove top of double boiler from heat, and beat about 5 more minutes, until stiff peaks form.

Super Delicious Chocolate Icing

⅓ cup buttermilk
¼ cup cocoa
6 tablespoons butter
1 (1-pound) box confectioners' sugar
1 teaspoon vanilla extract

In medium saucepan, bring buttermilk, cocoa, and butter to a boil. Gradually add confectioners' sugar and vanilla, blending until smooth and of spreading consistency.

Superman's chroniclers have portrayed him in a wide variety of artistic styles, but the basic details of his costume have remained substantially unchanged.

Superman wears a blue costume complemented by red trunks, red boots, and a long, flowing red cape. A yellow belt encircles his waist, and there is a highly stylized Superman insignia consisting of a large red letter "S," inscribed within a yellow shield with **five** sides, which is bordered in red and emblazoned on his chest. The back of Superman's cape bears a similar insignia.

The stylized "S" insignia on Superman's chest, small and sleek in Superman's earliest adventures, has become larger, more highly stylized, and more distinct throughout the course of his sixty-year career.

Mocha Icing

1 stick butter, softened
4 teaspoons strong coffee
3 tablespoons water
⅓ cup cocoa
1½ cups confectioners' sugar

Cream butter till fluffy. Stir in coffee and water; mix well. Blend cocoa with confectioners' sugar, then gradually add to butter mixture, blending until smooth and of spreading consistency.

Nutty Fudge Icing

½ cup margarine
1½ cups sugar
½ cup milk
¾ cup semisweet chocolate chips
1 cup chopped pecans

Bring margarine, sugar, and milk to a full rolling boil. Boil 2 minutes, remove from heat, then add chocolate and pecans. Blend quickly; beat until of spreading consistency. When mixture goes from shiny to dull (about 2 minutes), it's ready. Spread on a baked yellow or chocolate cake while cake is still warm.

Fast
and
Fabulous

FIVE ★ STAR

Cookies & Candies

Cocoa-Coconut Drops

²/₃ cup sweetened condensed milk
1½ cups shredded coconut
3 tablespoons cocoa
⅛ teaspoon salt
¼ teaspoon vanilla

Preheat oven to 350°. In medium bowl, combine ingredients until thoroughly blended. Drop by teaspoonfuls onto well-buttered baking sheet. Bake 15 minutes.

Nutty Cocoa Disks

Sort of a cookie-candy, this is quick and delicious.

1 cup semisweet chocolate chips
²/₃ cup condensed milk
1 cup chopped pecans
1 teaspoon vanilla extract
⅛ teaspoon salt

In a double boiler, melt chocolate chips and condensed milk together over hot water. Whisk until smooth. Remove from heat, then add remaining ingredients; stir well. Drop by teaspoonfuls onto well-greased baking pan. Bake at 350° for 9–11 minutes.

Chocolate Chip Easies

1 (18¼-ounce) box yellow cake mix
1 stick butter, softened
2 eggs
1 teaspoon vanilla extract
2 cups semisweet chocolate chips

Preheat oven to 350°. Mix together cake mix, butter, eggs, and vanilla with an electric mixer until well blended. Stir in chocolate chips. Drop by heaping spoonfuls onto buttered cookie sheets. Bake 11–15 minutes, until edges are golden. Cool in pan 2 minutes before removing to brown or parchment paper, which absorbs a little of the butter.

Chocolate Clouds

1 cup semisweet chocolate chips
3 egg whites
1 cup sifted confectioners' sugar
8 saltine crackers
½ teaspoon vanilla

Melt chocolate chips in microwave; stir until smooth, then allow to cool slightly. Beat egg whites until stiff but not dry. Gradually beat in sugar until stiff and satiny. Fold in cracker crumbs that have been finely crumbled in a food processor. Fold in chocolate and vanilla. Drop by teaspoonfuls onto greased baking sheets. Bake at 350° for 12–15 minutes. Makes 48 cookies.

Chocolate Nut Meringue Cookies

Easy, light, and delicious!

2 large egg whites
⅔ cup sugar
1 cup chopped pecans or walnuts
1 cup chocolate chips
1 teaspoon vanilla

Preheat oven to 350°. In mixer bowl, beat egg whites till foamy. Add sugar and beat till stiff. Add nuts, chips, and vanilla. Spoon teaspoonfuls onto ungreased cookie sheets. Turn oven off and place cookie sheets in; leave in oven several hours or overnight.

Every Muslim, male or female, must offer at least **five** daily prayers throughout the day.

1. The Early Morning Prayer (Salatu-I-Fajr), dawn to sunrise
2. The Noon Prayer (Salatu-z-Zuhr), after true noon until Mid-Afternoon prayer
3. The Mid-Afternoon Prayer (Salatu-I-Asr), after Noon prayer and until sunset
4. The Sunset Prayer (Salatu-I-Maghrib), after sunset until dusk
5. The Evening Prayer (Salatu-I-Isha), dusk until dawn, but pre-ferrably before mid-night

There are **five** books in the Jewish Torah: Genesis, Exodus, Leviticus, Numbers, and Deuteronomy.

The Torah is also known as the **Five Books of Moses** or the **Pentateuch** (Greek for "**five** containers," which refers to the scroll cases in which books were being kept).

The **five** books contain both a complete and ordered system of laws, as well as a historical description of the beginnings of what came to be known as Judaism.

Chocolate Crackle Cookies

½ cup butter-flavored shortening
2 eggs
1 tablespoon water
1 (18¼-ounce) box devil's food cake mix
1 cup confectioners' sugar

In a medium bowl, mix shortening, eggs, and water until well blended. Stir in cake mix, mixing until smooth. Roll dough into 1-inch balls, then roll in confectioners' sugar. Place balls 2 inches apart on cookie sheets. Bake 10 minutes in 375° oven. Dust cookies with sugar again before serving.

Brickle Sugar Cookies

These are so yummy!

1 (17.5-ounce) bag sugar cookie mix
1 stick butter (no substitutes), melted
1 extra large egg
1 tablespoon lightly packed brown sugar
½ (8-ounce) bag milk chocolate toffee bits (brickle)

Preheat oven to 350°. Stir cookie mix, melted butter, egg, and brown sugar together well; add brickle. Drop by teaspoonfuls on ungreased cookie sheet. Bake about 10 minutes or until golden brown around the edges. Makes about 27 (2-inch) cookies.

Lemon Chewies

Golden brown cookies with a chewy inside. Lemon-y delicious!

1 (18¼-ounce) box lemon cake mix
2 eggs
⅓ cup vegetable oil
1 teaspoon lemon extract
⅓ cup confectioners' sugar

Preheat oven to 375°. Mix cake mix with eggs, oil, and lemon extract until well blended. Drop dough by teaspoonfuls into a bowl of confectioners' sugar. Roll them around until they're lightly covered. Place on an ungreased cookie sheet. Bake 6–9 minutes, till golden.

Dainty Mint Chip Kisses

2 egg whites
¾ cup sugar
¼ teaspoon peppermint extract
2 drops green food coloring
1 (16-ounce) package mint chocolate chips

Preheat oven to 325°. Beat egg whites till stiff peaks form, then gradually add sugar. Gently stir in peppermint extract, green food coloring, and chocolate chips. Drop by teaspoonfuls onto cookie sheet. Put in preheated oven and turn off immediately. Leave in oven for several hours or overnight. Store in airtight tin. Yields 24.

Italian Almond Cookies

2 egg whites
Dash of salt
1 cup sugar
1 teaspoon almond extract
1 cup ground almonds

Line cookie sheets with parchment paper. Using electric mixer, beat egg whites till frothy. Add salt, then sugar, a tablespoon at a time, while beating on high speed till stiff peaks form. By hand, gently stir in almond extract and almonds. Drop by teaspoon onto prepared cookie sheets. Bake at 300° about 25 minutes, or until cookies are very lightly browned. When cool, peel cookies from paper and store in airtight tin. Makes about 30 cookies.

Easy Pastel Cookies

2 egg yolks
1 cup butter, softened
1 teaspoon vanilla extract
1 (18¼-ounce) box vanilla-flavored cake mix
⅓ cup granulated sugar for decoration

Preheat oven to 350°. In large mixing bowl, beat egg yolks and butter together well. Add vanilla. While beating, gradually add cake mix. Mixture should be stiff. If dough is sticky, refrigerate it 20–30 minutes.

Roll teaspoonfuls of dough into balls, then roll in sugar. Place on ungreased cookie sheets. Bake 11 minutes for soft cookies; 13 minutes for crispy cookies.

Editor's Extra: Fun to color the sugar by putting a few drops of food coloring with sugar in a zipper bag; shake till evenly coated. Great with other flavors of cake mix, too.

Potato Chip Cookies

These freeze exceptionally well.

1 cup butter, softened
½ cup sugar
1½ cups all-purpose flour
1 teaspoon vanilla extract
¾ cup finely crushed fresh potato chips

In large mixer bowl, beat butter and sugar till fluffy. Gradually add flour and beat again till smooth. By hand, add vanilla and potato chips; mix well. Drop by small teaspoonfuls onto ungreased cookie sheet. Bake in 325° oven 15–20 minutes, until light brown. Allow to cool, then sprinkle with sifted confectioners' sugar, if desired. Yields about 5 dozen.

Old-Fashioned Vinegar Cookies

2 sticks butter, softened
1 cup sugar
2 cups all-purpose flour
½ teaspoon baking soda
1 teaspoon vinegar

In medium mixing bowl, cream together butter and sugar. Gradually beat in flour, baking soda, and vinegar. Form dough into small balls, place on greased cookie sheets, and flatten with a fork. Bake at 350° for 8–10 minutes. Makes about 40 cookies.

In North America, telephone numbers with the prefix **555** are widely used for fictitious phone numbers in television shows, films, and other types of fictional media. In fact, only **555-0100** through **555-0199** are now specifically reserved for fictional use.

Phone companies started encouraging the use of the **555** prefix for fictional telephone numbers during the 1970s due to the many cases of people trying to call the numbers used. In older television shows from the 1950s or 1960s, **"KLondike 5"** or **"KLamath 5"** was used, as at the time the telephone exchanges used letters. (On American telephone dials, K and L are found on the number **5**.)

Some movie or television producers have acquired actual telephone numbers solely for the purpose of using them in a movie or on TV.

Touch of Bourbon Butter Cookies

1 cup butter, softened
1 cup sugar
1 egg
1 tablespoon bourbon
3 cups sifted all-purpose flour

In large mixing bowl, beat butter and sugar till fluffy.
Add egg and bourbon. Gradually add flour. Dough will
be stiff. Form into small balls, place on cookie sheet,
and flatten with a fork. Bake 12–15 minutes at 350°.
Remove immediately. Yields 6 dozen.

Editor's Extra: It makes a difference, so measure flour
after sifting.

Cream Cheese Delights

1 (3-ounce) package cream cheese, softened
½ stick butter, softened
1 cup sifted self-rising flour
½ cup apricot or raspberry jam
½ cup powdered sugar

In a medium bowl, beat cream cheese till fluffy. Add
butter and flour, and mix well. Divide dough in half.
Chill until firm.

Preheat oven to 350°. Roll out half the dough at a
time into ¼-inch thickness. Cut into small circles with
cookie cutter. Place ½ teaspoon jam in middle of each
cookie. Crimp sides to meet in middle. Bake on
ungreased cookie sheets at 350° for 20 minutes or
until lightly browned. Cool on racks. Dust with powdered sugar. Makes about 2 dozen.

Oh So Good
Peanut Butter Cookies

1 (18¼-ounce) box yellow cake mix with pudding
1 cup peanut butter
2 eggs
¼ cup sugar
¼ cup chopped honey roasted peanuts

Combine all ingredients in mixer bowl. Mix 2–3 minutes until well incorporated. Shape into walnut-size balls and place 2 inches apart on cookie sheets. With fork, press criss-cross pattern into cookies (wet your fork in water to keep from sticking). Bake in 350° oven 10–15 minutes. Cool slightly before removing from pan. Makes about 36 cookies.

Nutty Sugar Cookies

2 sticks butter, softened
1 cup sugar
1 teaspoon almond extract
2 cups all-purpose flour
1 cup chopped almonds

In medium mixing bowl, beat together butter, sugar, and almond extract till fluffy. Gradually add flour, then nuts, beating well. Shape dough into roll, wrap in wax paper, and refrigerate for a couple of hours.

Preheat oven to 325°. Slice roll into ¼-inch-thick cookies, and bake 20 minutes. Sprinkle hot cookies with additional sugar, if desired.

Whipped Shortbread

Great Christmas cookies. Makes plenty to share with family and friends.

3 cups butter, softened (no substitutes)
4½ cups all-purpose flour
1½ cups confectioners' sugar, sifted
1½ cups cornstarch
Halved candied cherries

Preheat oven to 300°. In very large mixing bowl, cream butter and sugar on medium speed till light and fluffy. Gradually add dry ingredients until well blended. With lightly floured hands, shape dough into 1-inch balls. Press lightly with floured fork. Top each cookie with a cherry half. Bake 20–22 minutes; do not let cookies brown. Makes 16–18 dozen.

Editor's Extra: Easy to third recipe, if desired.

Almond Handle Cookies

⅔ cup finely chopped almonds
½ cup sugar
½ cup butter or margarine
1 tablespoon all-purpose flour
2 tablespoons milk

In a medium skillet, combine almonds with remaining ingredients. Cook over medium heat till butter melts, then stir and remove from heat. Drop by half teaspoonfuls, 3 inches apart, onto greased baking sheet. Bake at 350° for 8 minutes, or until lightly browned. Cool slightly. Remove from baking sheet with broad spatula and roll around the handle of a wooden spoon. If cookies become hard on sheet, return to oven for a few minutes to soften. Makes 30 cookies.

Almond Stardust Meringues

¼ pound blanched almonds
3 egg whites
1 cup sifted confectioners' sugar
½ teaspoon grated lemon zest
½ teaspoon almond extract

Process almonds in food processor till finely chopped. Beat egg whites until stiff but not dry. Gradually add sugar; continue beating until mixture is completely blended, about 5 minutes. Stir in lemon zest, almond extract, and almonds. Drop by teaspoon onto well-greased and floured baking sheet. Bake at 275° for 30 minutes. Turn oven off, but leave cookies in oven at least ½ hour, or overnight. Makes about 4 dozen.

Editor's Extra: Blanched, in reference to almonds, means skinned—the almonds have been briefly put in boiling water so that their skins come off.

The perfect **fifth**, or **diapente**, is a musical interval that is responsible for the most consonant, or stable, harmony outside of the unison and octave, and is the basis for most western tuning systems. A helpful way to recognize a perfect **fifth** is to hum the starting of "Twinkle Twinkle Little Star," which is a familiar perfect **fifth**.

In musical notation, the staff is a set of **five** horizontal lines on which note symbols are placed to indicate pitch and rhythm. The lines are numbered from bottom to top; the bottom line is the first line and the top line is the **fifth** line.

Pecan Sandies

2 sticks butter, softened
¾ cup confectioners' sugar
1¼ cups chopped pecans
1 teaspoon vanilla
2 cups sifted all-purpose flour

Preheat oven to 325°. Cream together butter and sugar till fluffy. Stir in pecans and vanilla. Add flour a little at a time, stirring well. Form into cookies and place on ungreased cookie sheet. Bake 20 minutes. Remove from oven and allow to cool. Coat with extra confectioners' sugar before serving. Yields 3 dozen.

Brown Sugar Pecan Bites

1 packed cup brown sugar
1 egg white, slightly beaten
Pinch of salt
2 cups pecan halves
1 teaspoon vanilla extract

Preheat oven to 450° for 10 minutes. Blend together sugar, egg white, and salt. Stir in pecans and vanilla. Drop by teaspoonfuls onto well-greased baking sheet. Turn off oven before putting cookies in. Let sit in hot oven for 8 minutes.

Sesame Sensations

1 stick butter, softened
1/2 packed cup brown sugar
1 egg, separated
1 cup sifted all-purpose flour
1/3 cup sesame seeds

In medium bowl, cream butter and sugar together till fluffy. Stir in egg yolk, and mix well. Gradually add flour, and stir till a stiff dough forms. Shape dough into 1-inch balls. Whisk egg white till frothy; dip balls in beaten egg white, then roll in sesame seeds. Place on a lightly greased cookie sheet. Bake at 350° for 15–20 minutes. Makes 2 dozen.

Butter Oats Medallions

2/3 cup butter or margarine, softened
3 cups quick-cooking oats
1/2 cup sugar
1 egg, beaten
1 teaspoon almond extract

In a bowl, knead together butter, oats, and sugar into a solid mass. Add egg and almond extract and knead until a smooth dough is formed. Shape into balls the size of marbles. Place on greased baking sheet. Press tops of each ball down with tines of a fork. Bake at 325° for 10–15 minutes or until golden brown. Makes 2 1/2 dozen.

Shamrock Cookies

Bring out your baking artistry.

2 sticks butter, softened
1/2 cup sugar
1 egg yolk
1 teaspoon grated lemon rind
2 1/2 cups sifted all-purpose flour

Cream together butter and sugar until light and fluffy. Add egg yolk and lemon rind; mix well. Add flour gradually, until well incorporated. Shape dough into long thin rolls about 1/2 inch thick. Wrap in wax paper and chill about 30 minutes. Cut off thin slices of dough and place 4 slices together on a baking sheet, pressing down ends to resemble a four-leaf clover. Insert an additional small piece of dough to resemble a stem. Bake at 375° about 8 minutes, or until lightly browned around the edges. Makes about 6 dozen cookies.

Editor's Extra: Green food coloring makes these fun, and red clovers are pretty, too. Or sprinkle with green sugar granules.

Thanksgiving Gobbler Cookies

Kids love to help Mom make these for Thanksgiving!

1 package round, chocolate-striped cookies
(turkey tail)
1 cup chocolate frosting
24 miniature peanut butter cups
24 pieces candy corn
48 chocolate chips

With a sharp knife, cut 1/4 inch off one edge of cookies to make flat base (turkey tail). With chocolate frosting, glue large side of peanut butter cup over the hole in the middle of each cookie (turkey body). Then glue a corn candy in the middle of each peanut butter cup (gobbler). Next glue 2 chocolate chips on bottom of each peanut butter cup (legs). Makes 24.

Cut-Out Butter Cookies

2 sticks butter, melted
1 cup confectioners' sugar
1 egg, beaten
1 teaspoon vanilla
2¼ cups all-purpose flour

Cream butter, sugar, egg, and vanilla. Gradually stir in flour until well blended. Refrigerate, covered, at least 2 hours.

On a lightly floured surface, roll dough out ¼ inch thick. Using cookie cutters, cut into desired shapes. Bake on parchment-lined cookie sheets at 350° for 8–10 minutes. Cool on cookie sheets 5 minutes before transferring to a wire rack to cool completely.

German Chocolate Caramel Brownies

1 (14-ounce) bag caramels, unwrapped
1 (5-ounce) can evaporated milk, divided
1 (18¼-ounce) box German chocolate cake mix
¾ cup butter, melted
1 cup chocolate chips

In double boiler over simmering water, melt caramels with ½ can evaporated milk. Preheat oven to 350°. Combine cake mix with butter, remaining ½ can evaporated milk, and chocolate chips. Press ½ of dough into a greased 9x13-inch pan; top with caramel mixture. Spread evenly with remaining dough. Bake 30 minutes.

There are only **five** counties in the state of Rhode Island:

- Bristol
- Kent
- Newport
- Providence
- Washington

Connecticut became the **fifth** state to enter the Union on January 9, 1788.

Chocolate Rice Krispie Treats

8 cups Rice Krispies
½ stick butter
1 (20-ounce) package chocolate candy coating
¾ cup white corn syrup
2 teaspoons vanilla extract

Butter or spray a 9x13-inch pan. Place cereal in large bowl. In double boiler over simmering water, melt butter and chocolate with corn syrup, stirring occasionally. Remove from heat and add vanilla. Pour over cereal and stir well. Spoon mixture into prepared pan, and press down using buttered spatula. When cool, cut into squares. Makes about 40.

Chocolate Chip Caramel Yummies

1 (18-ounce) roll refrigerated chocolate chip cookie
    dough
32 vanilla caramels (unwrapped)
¼ cup evaporated milk
¼ teaspoon vanilla extract
1 cup semisweet chocolate chips

Preheat oven to 375°. Slice cookies ¼ inch thick. Press into bottom of greased 9x9-inch glass baking dish, forming an even crust. Bake 20–25 minutes. While cookies are baking, melt caramels with evaporated milk in double boiler over simmering water; remove from heat, then stir in vanilla. Sprinkle chocolate chips over warm cookie crust, then evenly pour caramel mixture over top. Chill until set, then cut into squares.

Chocolate Peanut Butter Bars

½ cup graham cracker crumbs
2½ cups confectioners' sugar
1 cup butter, melted
1 cup crunchy peanut butter
2 cups milk chocolate chips

In a medium mixing bowl, combine crumbs, sugar, butter, and peanut butter until well mixed. Spread in bottom of greased 9x13-inch glass baking dish. Microwave on HIGH 2 minutes. Remove and let sit. In a microwaveable bowl, melt chocolate. Stir well, then spread on peanut butter mixture while warm. Chill, then cut into bars.

Hazelnut Heaven Bars

2 egg whites
1 cup sugar
1 tablespoon all-purpose flour
1 teaspoon vanilla
1½ cups coarsely ground hazelnuts

Line a 9x13-inch baking dish with parchment paper. Beat egg whites till stiff. Gradually beat in sugar till stiff peaks form. Fold in flour. Cook in double boiler over boiling water about 3 minutes, stirring constantly. Remove from heat and blend in vanilla and nuts. Spread in prepared 9x13-inch pan. Bake at 350° for 15–20 minutes or until top looks dull. While warm, cut into bars. Cool slightly, then remove from pan. To remove paper, dampen it with cold water.

Just Like Heath Bars

2 cups all-purpose flour
1 cup butter, divided
1½ cups brown sugar, divided
1 cup chopped pecans
1 cup semisweet chocolate chips

Combine flour with ⅓ cup cold butter, and 1 cup brown sugar until finely crumbled. Spread mixture in bottom of greased 9x13-inch baking pan to form a crust. Sprinkle evenly with pecans. In small saucepan, cook remaining ⅔ cup butter and ½ cup brown sugar over medium heat, stirring constantly until entire surface boils rapidly. Remove from heat, and pour over pecans. Bake about 20 minutes. Remove from oven. While still hot, sprinkle evenly with chocolate chips; spread when melted. Cool, then cut into bars.

Toffee Bars

24 graham cracker squares
¾ cup butter
¾ cup packed brown sugar
Pinch of salt
¾ cup chopped pecans

Preheat oven to 350°. Line a 10x15-inch baking pan with foil. Arrange graham crackers in a single layer, with sides touching.

In a saucepan, heat butter, sugar, and salt until blended, about 2 minutes, stirring constantly. Remove from heat, and stir in pecans. Pour mixture evenly over graham crackers. Bake 10 minutes, then allow to cool 10 minutes. Cut into bars. Chill.

Moose Tracks

2 (18-ounce) rolls refrigerated chocolate chip cookie dough
1 cup chocolate-covered toffee bits
1 cup mini marshmallows
1 cup peanut butter chips
1 cup coarsely chopped salted peanuts

Preheat oven to 350°. In ungreased 9x13-inch pan, break up cookie dough. With floured fingers, press dough evenly in bottom of pan to form crust. Sprinkle with remaining ingredients; lightly press into dough. Bake 15–20 minutes or until golden brown. Cool completely on wire rack, about 30 minutes. Cut into bars.

Caramel-Coated Marshmallows

1 (10-ounce) package Rice Krispies
1 (14-ounce) package caramels, unwrapped
1 (14-ounce) can sweetened condensed milk
1 stick butter
1 (16-ounce) package marshmallows

Line a baking sheet with wax paper. Place cereal in medium bowl. In double boiler over simmering water, melt caramels with milk and butter, stirring occasionally; remove from heat. Using a fork or skewer, quickly dip marshmallows into caramel mixture, then roll in cereal. Place on prepared baking sheet; chill 30 minutes. Store in airtight container in refrigerator.

The expression "**five by five**" originates from the U.S. Military and refers to the measurement on a level of one to **five** for signal strength and signal clarity in a radio transmission—one being the worst, and **five** being the best. The **fifth** and highest level for each being, "Loud" and "Clear" respectively. Thus "**five by five**" was adapted to define anything ideal.

The Grammy Awards ceremony has grown over the past forty years. Only thirteen awards were given out in 1958, and more than thirty major awards are presented now. Among the categories that have been added over the years are Rock and Roll, Rap, New Age Music, Reggae and Music Videos.

The 48th Annual Grammy Awards (2006) was dominated by rock band U2, winning **five** awards:

- Best Rock Album
- Album of the Year
- Best Rock Song
- Best Rock Performance by a Duo or Group with Vocal
- Song of the Year

Other artists who have won **five** awards in a single year are:

- Alicia Keyes, 2002
- Nora Jones, 2003
- Beyoncé Knowles, 2004
- Lauryn Hill, 1999
- Roger Miller, 1965

Time-Tested Rocky Road

1 (12-ounce) package chocolate chips
1 (14-ounce) can sweetened condensed milk
2 tablespoons butter
1 (10½-ounce) package miniature marshmallows
1 (8-ounce) jar unsalted roasted peanuts

Line bottom and sides of a 9x13-inch pan with wax paper. Cook chocolate chips, condensed milk, and butter in a saucepan over low heat till chocolate is melted; remove from heat. In a medium bowl, combine marshmallows and peanuts. Stir in chocolate mixture until mixed well. Pour into a 9x13-inch pan. Chill 2 hours or till firm. Remove from pan, peel off wax paper, and cut into 1-inch squares with a wet knife. If desired, wrap pieces in plastic wrap. Makes about 8 dozen.

Peanut Butter Cornflake Candy

An old favorite!

1 cup sugar
1 cup corn syrup
1 (12-ounce) jar crunchy peanut butter
1 teaspoon vanilla extract
6 cups cornflakes

In large nonstick saucepan, bring sugar and corn syrup to a boil. Add peanut butter and vanilla, and stir well. Add cornflakes, one cup at a time, and mix to coat. Drop by tablespoon onto wax paper.

Sour Cream Candy

3 cups brown sugar
1 cup sour cream
1 stick butter (no substitutes)
1 teaspoon vanilla extract
1 cup chopped walnuts

Butter a 9x13-inch glass dish. Cook sugar and sour cream in medium saucepan over medium-high heat to soft-ball stage (240° on candy thermometer). Remove from heat, and add butter. Beat until mixture gets grainy looking. Stir in vanilla and nuts; pour into prepared dish. Allow to set, then cut into squares.

Make Your Own Creamy Caramels

2 cups sugar
1 cup light corn syrup
2 cups heavy cream, divided
½ teaspoon salt
½ teaspoon vanilla

Butter a 9x13-inch dish. In a heavy 3-quart saucepan, cook sugar, corn syrup, and 1 cup cream over medium-high heat about 10 minutes, stirring constantly. Insert candy thermometer. From this point on, stir only if necessary to prevent scorching. Very slowly, add remaining 1 cup cream, being sure not to stop the boiling. When thermometer reaches 230°, lower heat and cook slowly to 244°. Remove from heat, then add salt and vanilla; stir only to mix. Pour into prepared dish. When cool, cut into squares; wrap pieces in wax paper.

Fun Pretzel Rolos

60 mini pretzels
1 (13-ounce) package Rolo candies
20 pecan halves
20 M&Ms
20 candy corn candies

Line cookie sheet with foil. Place pretzels on foil. Top each pretzel with a Rolo. Bake at 250° for 4 minutes (candies will retain their shape). Place pecan halves, M&Ms, and candy corn on top of Rolos, and press down so candy fills pretzel. Cool slightly. Refrigerate 10 minutes.

The Best Pecan Log Roll

1 cup butterscotch chips
⅓ cup sweetened condensed milk
½ teaspoon vanilla
1 cup chopped pecans, divided
1 egg white, slightly beaten

Melt butterscotch chips in double boiler over simmering water. Remove from heat, then add condensed milk, vanilla, and ½ cup pecans; stir well. Refrigerate until firm enough to handle. Spread onto wax paper, and form a 12-inch roll. Brush with egg white, then roll in remaining pecans. Refrigerate until firm, then slice.

Oreo Fudge Squares

20 Oreos, broken into chunks, divided
1 (14-ounce) can sweetened condensed milk
2 tablespoons butter
2⅔ cups white chocolate chips
1 teaspoon vanilla extract

Line sides and bottom of 2-quart glass baking dish with buttered wax paper. Cover bottom of dish with ½ the Oreos. In a medium saucepan over low heat, cook milk, butter, and chips until chips are melted; stir well. Remove from heat, then stir in vanilla. Pour over Oreos. Sprinkle with remaining Oreos. Chill, covered, 1 hour. Cut into small squares.

Easy Breezy Microwave Fudge

1 (1-pound) box confectioners' sugar
½ cup cocoa
¼ cup milk
1 stick butter
1 teaspoon vanilla

Blend sugar and cocoa in a microwaveable bowl; stir in milk. Place slices of butter on top of mixture and microwave on HIGH 2 minutes. Remove from microwave and stir well. Stir in vanilla. Spread onto wax paper-lined pan. Chill 1 hour, then cut into squares.

Shakira was the night's big winner at the 7th Annual Latin Grammy Awards (2006), winning **five** awards. She is the first female recording artist to win Album of the Year.

No Bake Chocolate Cream Cheese Fudge

4 ounces unsweetened chocolate
1 (8-ounce) package cream cheese, softened
4 cups confectioners' sugar
½ cup chopped nuts
1 teaspoon vanilla

Melt chocolate. In large mixing bowl, cream together cream cheese and confectioners' sugar. Stir in melted chocolate, nuts, and vanilla; mix well. Pour into a well-buttered 8x8-inch pan, and chill until firm. Cut into small squares.

Creamy Peanut Butter Fudge

This is super easy, and so delicious!

¾ cup evaporated milk
2 cups sugar
1 cup creamy peanut butter
1 cup marshmallow crème
1 teaspoon vanilla

In medium saucepan over medium heat, cook milk and sugar until soft-ball stage (236°–240°). Remove from heat. Quickly stir in peanut butter, marshmallow crème, and vanilla. Pour into a buttered 2-quart baking dish. When firm, cut into squares.

Creamy Chocolate Fudge

This is what fudge should taste like . . . fantastic! And so easy.

2 cups semisweet chocolate chips
½ bar unsweetened baking chocolate, chopped
1 (14-ounce) can sweetened condensed milk
2 teaspoons vanilla extract
1 cup chopped nuts

Melt chocolate with condensed milk in double boiler over hot water. Remove from heat; stir in vanilla and nuts. Spread fudge evenly in wax paper-lined, 2-quart baking dish. Chill until set, about 2 hours.

Divinity

2 egg whites
2½ cups sugar
½ cup light corn syrup
½ cup water
½ teaspoon vanilla

Beat egg whites till stiff. Cook sugar, syrup, and water to thin syrup (soft-ball) stage. Slowly pour ⅓ of mixture over stiffly beaten egg whites, beating constantly. Cook remaining syrup to hard-ball stage (310°). Add to egg mixture with vanilla, beating till mixture holds shape and will drop from a spoon. Drop by spoonfuls onto wax paper.

The Academy Awards, known as the Oscars, have been presented annually since 1927 by the Academy of Motion Picture Arts and Sciences.

Only three films have won the top **five** Academy awards (Best Picture, Best Director, Best Actor, Best Actress, and Best Screenplay):

- *It Happened One Night* (1934)
- *One Flew Over The Cuckoo's Nest* (1975)
- *The Silence of the Lambs* (1991)

Films that won **five** awards including Best Picture:

- *Gladiator* (2000)
- *Oliver!* (1968)
- *Terms of Endearment* (1983)

Films that have won **five** Oscars without winning Best Picture:

- *Wilson* (1944)
- *The Bad and the Beautiful* (1952)
- *The King and I* (1956)
- *Mary Poppins* (1964)
- *Doctor Zhivago* (1965)
- *Who's Afraid of Virginia Woolf?* (1966)
- *Saving Private Ryan* (1998)
- *The Aviator* (2004)

Pralines in Minutes

So nice at holiday time, these will become a Christmas tradition . . . especially since they can be whipped up in minutes.

1 cup light brown sugar
1 cup sugar
5 tablespoons water
2 tablespoons butter
1½ cups chopped pecans

Butter a 3-foot strip of wax paper. In a large saucepan, cook sugars, water, and butter over high heat. When mixture begins to boil rapidly, add pecans. Boil, stirring constantly, until mixture forms large bubbles on top and looks sugary, 3–4 minutes. Remove from heat; drop quickly by spoonfuls onto prepared wax paper. Makes about 24.

Editor's Extra: Pralines should be spooned onto wax paper quickly when near soft-ball stage . . . too soon and they won't set . . . too late and they sugar. But you can always put them back in the pot to cook a minute longer, or to "unsugar" by adding a tablespoon of water. Once you get the feel of it, you'll know when it's time.

Fast
and
Fabulous

FIVE ★ STAR

Pies & Other Desserts

The Great Highland Bagpipe, probably the best-known variety of bagpipe, is comprised of an air bag, usually made of sheepskin, into which are bound **five** pipes: a bass drone, two tenor drones, the mouthpiece, and the chanter on which the tune is played.

The Great Highland Bagpipe is classified as a woodwind instrument, like the bassoon, oboe, or clarinet, although its design is decidedly different from any other instrument.

Ole Buttermilk Pie

A custard pie never tasted so good.

1 refrigerated pie dough for single crust
1 cup sugar
2½ tablespoons flour
2 eggs
1¾ cups buttermilk

Preheat oven to 350°. Pierce pie crust with a fork all over, and prebake for 5 minutes. Whisk remaining ingredients together and pour into pie crust; bake 50–60 minutes till somewhat browned in the middle.

Editor's Extra: You can whisk in a pat of soft butter and/or a teaspoon of vanilla to make a richer pie, but this one is a basic winner . . . any way you slice it.

Marshmallow Cheesecake Pie

3 (8-ounce) packages cream cheese, softened
1 (7½-ounce) jar marshmallow crème
2 eggs
3 tablespoons flour
1 (9-inch) graham cracker crust

Preheat oven to 350°. In mixing bowl, beat cream cheese, marshmallow crème, eggs, and flour until smooth; pour into crust. Bake 45 minutes or until edges are brown. Turn oven off, and leave in oven for 1 hour. Remove to wire rack to finish cooling. Chill at least 4 hours before serving.

Bailey's Marshmallow Pie

½ cup milk
1 (10½-ounce) bag large marshmallows
⅓ cup Bailey's Irish Cream
1½ cups heavy cream
1 chocolate cookie pie crust

Heat milk and marshmallows in large saucepan over medium heat, stirring constantly, till marshmallows melt. Pour mixture into large mixing bowl, and chill 30–45 minutes, stirring occasionally.

Add Bailey's 1 tablespoon at a time to marshmallow mixture, stirring well after each addition. Beat heavy cream in medium mixing bowl till stiff. Fold cream into marshmallow mixture. Pour into pie crust, then cover and chill about 4 hours. Refrigerate leftovers.

Creamy Pineapple Pie

⅓ cup sugar
1 (8-ounce) package cream cheese, softened
1 (20-ounce) can crushed pineapple, drained well
1 (8-ounce) tub frozen whipped topping, thawed
1 graham cracker pie crust

Cream sugar and cream cheese till fluffy; combine pineapple and whipped topping. Mix ingredients together well, and pour into the pie crust. Cover and refrigerate at least 30 minutes before serving.

Editor's Extra: Great to sub a vanilla wafer crust, too.

Tropical Cream Pie

A light and refreshing dessert, and so simple to make. You'll love this!

2 (3-ounce) boxes coconut instant pudding
4 cups cold milk
1 shortbread cookie pie crust
2 bananas, sliced, sprinkled with lemon juice
1 pint whipping cream, whipped

Combine pudding with milk, and prepare according to package directions. Spoon into pie crust. Top with sliced bananas. Top bananas with whipped cream.

Editor's Extra: Pretty to garnish top with toasted coconut.

Scrumptious Strawberry Pie

Impress your friends with this scrumptious dessert.

1 (14-ounce) can sweetened condensed milk
⅓ cup fresh lemon juice
1 (12-ounce) container frozen Cool Whip, thawed
1 quart fresh strawberries, washed, sliced
1 (9-inch) pie crust, baked

Whisk milk and lemon juice together till thick; stir in Cool Whip. Gently fold in sliced strawberries. Spoon into baked pie crust. Chill thoroughly (3–4 hours) before serving. Serves 8.

Chris Sikorski's Blueberry Pie

1 (8-ounce) package cream cheese, softened
1½ cups powdered sugar
1 (8-ounce) tub frozen whipped topping, thawed
1 pint blueberries
1 graham cracker crust

Beat cream cheese until fluffy. Slowly add powdered sugar, and continue beating. Fold in whipped topping and blueberries. Pour into graham cracker crust. Refrigerate until set.

Summertime Lemon Pies

Need dessert in a hurry? This takes very little time to prepare!

1 (8-ounce) package cream cheese, softened
1 (6-ounce) can frozen lemonade concentrate, thawed
1 (14-ounce) can sweetened condensed milk
1 (12-ounce) container frozen Cool Whip, thawed
2 graham cracker pie crusts

In large bowl, beat cream cheese until fluffy. Stir in lemonade and condensed milk, mixing well. Gently stir in Cool Whip. Spread into pie crusts. Refrigerate several hours before serving.

Lemon Ice Box Pie

1 (14-ounce) can sweetened condensed milk
3 eggs, separated
Juice of 2 or 3 lemons
1 graham cracker crust
2 tablespoons sugar

Mix together condensed milk, egg yolks, and lemon juice. Pour into crust. Beat egg whites till stiff peaks form, gradually adding sugar. Put meringue on top of pie, and bake in 350° oven till top is lightly browned, about 5 minutes.

Editor's Extra: If you're watching your fat intake, substitute fat-free condensed milk, and use Egg Beaters instead of egg yolks.

A **fifth column** is a group of people that secretly undermines a larger group to which it is expected to be loyal, such as a nation. The term originated with a 1936 radio address by Emilio Mola, a nationalist general during the 1936–39 Spanish Civil War. As four of his army columns (formations) moved on Madrid, the general referred to his militant supporters within the capital as his "**fifth column**," intent on undermining the Republican government from within.

The Ultimate Margarita Pie

1 (8-ounce) package cream cheese, softened
2 packages dry margarita mix
⅔ cup sugar
1 (8-ounce) carton frozen whipped topping, thawed
1 (9-inch) graham cracker crust

Beat cream cheese until fluffy. Combine cream cheese, margarita mix, and sugar; mix until smooth. Gently fold in whipped topping. Spread into crust, and freeze until ready to serve.

Editor's Extra: Garnish with lime slices. I like to sprinkle a few crushed pretzels on top to give it a hint of salt like on the rim of a margarita.

Tiny Key Lime Pies

2 Key limes
1 (8-ounce) package cream cheese, softened
½ cup sugar
1 egg, beaten
6 miniature graham cracker pie shells

Preheat oven to 325°. Grate 1 teaspoon lime zest into mixing bowl. Squeeze 3 tablespoons juice into same mixing bowl. Add cream cheese and beat till creamy. Stir in sugar and egg, beating till fluffy. Evenly divide mixture between pie shells. Bake 30 minutes, or till knife inserted in center comes out clean. Cool slightly, then refrigerate until ready to serve. Garnish with additional lime zest. Serves 6.

Light and Creamy Peanut Butter Pie

1 (8-ounce) package cream cheese, softened
½ cup peanut butter, smooth or crunchy
1 cup powdered sugar
1 (8-ounce) carton frozen Cool Whip, thawed
1 graham cracker crust

Cream the cream cheese in mixer; beat in peanut butter till smooth, then powdered sugar till smooth. Fold in Cool Whip, and pile on crust. Freeze or refrigerate.

Editor's Extra: Keep Dream Whip on hand; it's a good substitute when you're out of Cool Whip. This is light and fluffy with two packets whipped with milk.

Creamy Candy Bar Pie

18 big marshmallows
1 stick butter
1 (6-pack [9.3-ounces]) Hershey's candy bars, broken
½ pint whipping cream, whipped
1 graham cracker crust

In double boiler, melt marshmallows and butter. Add Hershey's bars, and stir until chocolate is melted. Cool slightly, then add whipped cream. Spread into crust and chill several hours before serving. Serves 8.

The first U.S. postage stamps were issued on July 1, 1847. At that time, postal rates varied by distance traveled: under 300 miles, letters cost **five cents** per half ounce; over 300 miles, letters cost ten cents per half ounce. The first stamps issued were engraved **five-cent** red-brown stamps depicting Benjamin Franklin (the first postmaster of the United States), and ten-cent stamps in black featuring George Washington.

The post office had become so efficient by 1851 that Congress was able to reduce the common rate to three cents (which remained unchanged for over a century), necessitating a new issue of stamps. Values included a one, three, **five**, ten, and twelve-cent stamp.

Perforation was introduced in 1857, and self-stick stamps came about in 1974.

Five nations, a confederacy of the Huron-Iroquois Indians, consisted of five tribes: Mohawks, Onondagas, Cayugas, Oneidas, and Senecas. (After 1722 they were joined by the Tuscarora.) They inhabited the region which is now the state of New York. The spiritual union of the nations began before European contact, with a constitution recorded with special beads called wampum, which served the same purpose as money in other cultures.

Anthropologists speculate that this constitution was created sometime between the middle 1400s and early 1600s, but other scholars who account for Iroquois oral tradition argue that the event took place as early as 1100. The Iroquois political union and democratic government have been credited as possible influences on the United States Constitution.

Really Easy Mocha Chocolate Pie

1 (3-ounce) box cook and serve chocolate pudding
3 teaspoons instant coffee
1½ cups milk
1 cup heavy cream, whipped
1 (8-inch) pie shell, baked

Mix pudding mix, instant coffee, and milk in a saucepan. Cook and stir over medium heat until mixture comes to a full boil. Remove from heat. Cool 5 minutes, stirring once or twice. Fold in ½ the whipped cream. Pour into pie shell. Chill well before serving. Make a border with remaining whipped cream. Serves 6–8.

Krispie Cream Pie

The perfect complement to any meal!

2 tablespoons butter
1 (12-ounce) package chocolate chips
2½ cups Rice Krispies
1 quart coffee ice cream, softened
Shaved unsweetened chocolate for garnish

In medium microwaveable bowl, melt butter and chocolate chips. Remove from microwave, and stir in Rice Krispies. Spread evenly into a buttered 9-inch deep-dish pie plate. Chill well. Spread ice cream in crust. Freeze 6 hours. Garnish with chocolate shavings before serving. Serves 8.

Malted Milk Ball Pie

This is absolutely fabulous!

1 pint vanilla ice cream, softened
2 cups crushed malted milk balls, divided
1 (9-inch) graham cracker crust
⅓ cup marshmallow crème
1 (8-ounce) carton frozen Cool Whip, thawed

Mix ice cream and ¾ cup crushed malted milk balls. Spread into crust. Freeze.

Combine marshmallow crème, ¾ cup crushed malted milk balls, and whipped topping. Spread over frozen ice cream mixture. Freeze again.

Just before serving, top with remaining ½ cup crushed malted milk balls.

Surprise Pecan Pie

Makes its own crust!

⅔ cup egg whites
1 cup sugar
½ teaspoon baking powder
1 cup chopped pecans
½ cup crushed Ritz Crackers

Beat egg whites until soft peaks form. Combine sugar and baking powder, and gradually add to egg whites a tablespoon at a time, beating until stiff peaks form. Gently stir in pecans and cracker crumbs. Bake in greased (or buttered) pie pan about 45 minutes at 300°. Allow to cool. Top with whipped cream, if desired. Serves 8.

Simply Southern Peach Cobbler

1 cup sugar
1 cup self-rising flour
¾ cup water
1 stick margarine
1 (28-ounce) can peaches, drained

Preheat oven to 400°. Mix sugar and flour in a bowl. Gradually stir in water to form a batter. In a 2-quart glass baking dish, melt margarine. Pour batter over butter. Do not stir. Evenly distribute peaches over top. Sprinkle cinnamon on top, if desired. Bake 50–60 minutes, until crust is golden brown.

Cinnamon Apple Crumble

1 cup brown sugar
¾ cup Bisquick
1 tablespoon cinnamon
½ stick butter, melted
8–10 medium apples, peeled, sliced

Preheat oven to 350°. Butter a 9x13-inch glass baking dish. Combine sugar, Bisquick, cinnamon, and butter until crumbly. Layer apples in bottom of baking dish. Sprinkle with sugar mixture. Bake about 30 minutes. Serves 8.

Oatmeal Apple Crisp

⅔ cup firmly packed brown sugar
½ cup sifted all-purpose flour
1 cup maple-flavored instant oatmeal
½ cup butter or margarine, melted
1 (21-ounce) can apple pie filling

Preheat oven to 350°. Blend together dry ingredients; stir in melted butter. Press ⅔ of mixture into a lightly buttered 8-inch-square cake pan. Cover with pie filling. Sprinkle with remaining dry mixture. Bake for 30–35 minutes, until lightly browned. Cut into squares when cool. Serve with ice cream or whipped cream, if desired.

Cherry Nut Crisp

1 (21-ounce) can cherry pie filling
1 (18¼-ounce) box orange cake mix
1 cup chopped pecans
1 tablespoon brown sugar/cinnamon mixture
1 stick butter, melted

Spoon cherry pie filling in the bottom of a greased 9x13-inch baking dish. Top with dry cake mix, pecans, and brown sugar/cinnamon mixture. Drizzle butter evenly over top. Bake in 350° oven 35–45 minutes. Serve with vanilla ice cream or whipped cream, if desired.

Epsilon is the **fifth** letter of the Greek alphabet. In the system of Greek numerals, it has a value of **five**. The lower-case letter is used as in mathematics as the symbol meaning a very small, insignificant, or negligible quantity of something.

In astronomy, Epsilon usually denotes the **fifth** brightest star in a constellation.

The hobo **nickel** is a sculptural art form involving the creative modification of small-denomination coins, usually the **nickel**, because of its size, thickness, and relative softness. Due to its low cost and portability, this medium was particularly popular among hobos, hence the name.

Some 100,000–200,000 classic hobo nickels were carved from 1913–1980. The Original Hobo **Nickel** Society (OHNS) was created in 1992 for collectors. Nice classic old hobo nickels were worth $10–$50 each in the 1980s, but rose in value to $100–$1000 each by the mid-1990s.

Modern artists have created altered **nickels** in such large quantities that, within the next few years, the number of modern carvings is expected to surpass that of classic old hobo **nickels**. Most of the classic old hobo **nickels** are not yet in the hands of collectors, whereas almost all modern carvings are.

Delicious Blueberry Dessert

1 (20-ounce) can crushed pineapple, undrained
1 (18¼-ounce) box butter-flavored cake mix
3 cups fresh or frozen blueberries
⅔ cup sugar
½ cup butter, melted

Preheat oven to 350°. Butter a 9x13-inch pan. Spoon pineapple in bottom. Top with dry cake mix, then blueberries and sugar. Drizzle butter evenly over top. Bake about 45 minutes, or until bubbly.

Cherry Cheese Pastries

1 cup cherry pie filling, divided
½ teaspoon vanilla extract
1 (8-count) can crescent rolls
½ (8-ounce) package cream cheese, softened, divided
½ cup vanilla frosting

Preheat oven to 375°. Mix pie filling with vanilla extract. Separate crescent rolls into 4 rectangles. Place on cookie sheet; seal perforations. Spread each rectangle with 2 tablespoons cream cheese, then top with ¼ cup cherry pie filling. Bake 10–12 minutes or until lightly browned. Remove from oven immediately. Heat frosting in microwave 15–20 seconds; drizzle over warm pastries. Serve warm.

Hobo Nickel

Cherry Pie Roll-Ups

1 (21-ounce) can cherry pie filling (or fruit of choice)
8 large flour tortillas
1½ cups water
1½ cups sugar
⅔ cup butter

Spoon pie filling equally down center of each tortilla. Roll up, and place seam side down in a large baking dish. In a saucepan, bring water, sugar, and butter to a boil. Pour over filled tortillas. Chill for an hour or more (or overnight).

Bake in 350° oven about 20 minutes, till bubbly.

Editor's Extra: For a crispy exterior, sprinkle with more sugar, and run under the broiler for a few minutes.

Baked Apples with Praline Topping

½ cup apple juice
¼ teaspoon ground cinnamon, divided
¼ cup coarsely chopped pecans or walnuts
¼ cup packed brown sugar
4 small red baking apples, cored

Combine apple juice and ⅛ teaspoon cinnamon in a small bowl. In another small bowl, combine nuts, brown sugar, and remaining cinnamon. Remove peel from top of each apple. Pour apple juice mixture into a 2-quart baking dish. Place apples in apple juice mixture. Sprinkle nut mixture over apples. Bake covered at 350° for 35–40 minutes.

Disappearing Cream Puffs

Serve them to guests, and watch them disappear.

2 cups milk
¾ cup butter
Dash of salt
2 cups sifted all-purpose flour
6 large eggs

Bring milk and butter to a fast boil in a medium saucepan. Remove from heat. Add salt and flour, stirring constantly, until mixture forms a ball; cool. In large mixing bowl, mix dough with eggs, one at a time, beating constantly at slow speed until each egg is thoroughly incorporated. Drop by tablespoon onto greased and floured baking sheet. Bake at 375° for 45 minutes or until golden brown. Do not open oven door during cooking. Cool. Split puffs only enough to fill with ice cream, whipped cream, or pudding.

Oreo Ice Cream Dessert

1 package Oreos, crushed, divided
1 stick butter, melted
½ gallon vanilla ice cream, softened, divided
2 (10-ounce) jars hot fudge sauce, divided
1 (12-ounce) carton frozen Cool Whip, thawed

Reserve ½ cup Oreos. Mix remaining Oreos with butter, and press onto bottom of 9x13-inch pan. Spread half of ice cream over Oreos. Top with 1 jar fudge sauce. Spread remaining ice cream over fudge sauce. Pour remaining fudge sauce over top. Spread with Cool Whip, and garnish with reserved Oreos.

Rich Chocolate Mousse

⅔ cup milk
2 tablespoons sugar
2 tablespoons hazelnut liqueur (Frangelico)
1 large egg, beaten
1 cup semisweet chocolate chips

Heat milk; set aside. In blender container, combine sugar, liqueur, egg, and chocolate chips till smooth. Add hot milk while blending. Pour into small coffee cups; top with whipped cream, if desired.

Vanilla Chiffon Pudding

1 envelope unflavored gelatin
¼ cup sugar, divided
2 eggs, separated
1¾ cups milk
1 teaspoon vanilla extract

In small saucepan, mix gelatin and 2 tablespoons sugar; blend in egg yolks and milk. Let stand 1 minute. Cook, stirring occasionally, over low heat until gelatin is completely dissolved, about 5 minutes. Stir in vanilla. Pour into large bowl and chill, stirring occasionally, until mixture mounds slightly when dripped from a spoon.

Beat egg whites until soft peaks form. Gradually add remaining sugar and beat until stiff. Gently fold into gelatin mixture. Refrigerate until set. Serves 8.

The Famous Five are a group of child detectives—four children and a dog—created by British children's author Enid Blyton (1897–1968) in the 1940s. Three of the children, Julian, Dick, and Anne, are siblings. Georgina, their cousin, is a tomboy always known as "George," who has a dog named Timmy.

The stories are set in rural England, and always take place during the children's holidays. The characters are featured in about thirty-one titles. Her books were immensely popular in Britain and Australia, and were translated into forty languages, including Spanish, French, Japanese, and Hebrew.

The Famous Five launched a 1978 television series that had twenty-six, thirty-minute episodes on BBC.

French Vanilla Custard

3 cups milk
1 (3-ounce) box French vanilla instant pudding mix
½ cup sugar
1 teaspoon vanilla
1 (8-ounce) carton frozen whipped topping, thawed

Combine milk, pudding mix, sugar, and vanilla, and stir until smooth. Fold in whipped topping. Chill until set. Serve in pretty dishes or stemware.

Editor's Extra: A splash of apricot brandy over each serving gives this dish an interesting flavor.

Classic Crème Brûlée

2 cups whipping cream
4 egg yolks, separated
2½ tablespoons sugar
1 teaspoon vanilla
½ cup brown sugar

Preheat oven to 325°. Heat whipping cream over low heat until hot, not boiling. Beat egg yolks, gradually adding granulated sugar. Remove cream from heat and pour into egg mixture very slowly, stirring constantly to prevent curdling. Add vanilla. Pour into an 8-inch square casserole dish. Place in larger pan of water, and bake uncovered about 45 minutes, or until a knife inserted in center comes out clean.

Sprinkle with brown sugar. Place under broiler for about a minute or until sugar caramelizes. Chill several hours before serving. Serves 6.

Peachy Brûlée

Delicious and beautiful!

4 fresh peaches, peeled, sliced thick
4 tablespoons gourmet red raspberry sauce
1 cup whipping cream
2 teaspoons vanilla
1 cup dark brown sugar

Drain peaches for a couple hours. Place in deep pie dish. Drizzle raspberry sauce over peaches. Beat whipping cream and vanilla until stiff peaks form. Spread over peaches. Refrigerate, covered. Two hours before serving, place dish in freezer to harden.

At serving time, preheat broiler. Remove dessert from freezer and sprinkle top with brown sugar, covering cream completely. Place 4–5 inches below source of heat. Broil 2–3 minutes or just until top is hot and glistening. Serve while hot.

Perfect Peach Delight

1 (3-ounce) package cream cheese, softened
⅓ cup lemon juice
1 (14-ounce) can sweetened condensed milk
1 (21-ounce) can peach pie filling
¼ cup whipped cream

Cream together cream cheese, lemon juice, and sweetened condensed milk until well blended. Spoon a layer of cheese mixture into 4 parfait glasses. Top with a layer of pie filling. Repeat layering until glasses are full. Garnish with whipped cream. Keep chilled until serving time.

Editor's Extra: Can be also made in a graham or baked pie crust.

Banana Popsicles

3 or 4 bananas, peeled, halved
3 tablespoons orange juice
1 (6-ounce) bag semisweet chocolate chips
1 tablespoon butter
1 cup finely chopped pecans

Insert wooden sticks into each banana. Brush bananas with orange juice. Place on wax paper-lined cookie sheet, and freeze until firm.

Melt chocolate chips and butter in microwave; stir to blend. Cool slightly, then spoon over frozen bananas. Immediately roll in chopped nuts. Keep in freezer until serving time.

Bananas in Kahlúa Sauce

⅛ cup light brown sugar
⅛ cup sugar
6 large bananas, sliced
½ cup Kahlúa liqueur
¼ cup butter

Caramelize sugars in hot (dry) sauté pan (be careful not to burn the sugar). Remove pan from heat. Add bananas, Kahlúa, and butter, and stir until butter is melted. This tastes great alone or served over ice cream.

Blueberry Parfaits

1 cup shortbread cookie crumbs
3 tablespoons butter, melted
1 cup lemon curd
1 cup frozen whipped topping, thawed
2 cups blueberries

Mix cookie crumbs and melted butter. Layer 2 table-spoons crumb mixture into each of 4 parfait glasses. Then layer with 2 tablespoons lemon curd, 2 table-spoons whipped topping, and ¼ cup blueberries in each glass, repeating layers until glasses are full. Keep chilled until serving time.

Chocolate Waffles on a Stick

What's not to love! These are fabulous.

1 cup semisweet chocolate chips
1 cup milk chocolate chips
2 teaspoons shortening
5 frozen Belgian waffles
1 Heath bar, crushed

Melt chocolate chips and shortening over medium heat, stirring constantly. Toast waffles according to package directions. Cut waffles in half crosswise. Insert a wooden skewer into each piece. Dip waffles in chocolate to coat, allowing excess to drip back into pan. Place on a wax paper-lined baking sheet. Sprinkle with crushed Heath bar. Refrigerate until chocolate is set.

TV's top **five** longest running fictional series in the United States are:

1. *Gunsmoke,*
   633 episodes
   (1955–1975)
2. *Lassie,*
   588 episodes
   (1954–1973)
3. *Death Valley Days,*
   452 episodes
   (1952–1972)
4. *Ozzie and Harriett*
   435 episodes
   (1952–1966)
5. *Bonanza,*
   430 episodes
   (1959–1972)

The top **five** daily newspapers in the United States (by circulation, as of March 2006) are:

1. *USA Today*–
   2,528,437
2. *Wall Street Journal*–
   2,058,342
3. *New York Times*–
   1,683,855
4. *Los Angeles Times*–
   1,231,318
5. *Washington Post*–
   960,684

Chocolate-Coated Strawberries

Always a hit!

¾ pound white chocolate
½ pound milk chocolate
¼ pound semisweet chocolate
2 tablespoons vegetable oil, divided
1 quart strawberries

Place chocolate in 3 separate microwaveable bowls with 1 tablespoon oil in white chocolate, 2 teaspoons oil in milk chocolate, and 1 teaspoon oil in semisweet chocolate. Microwave white chocolate and oil until chocolate is melted, stirring to blend. Dip berries in white chocolate to coat ¾ way up berry. Allow coating to harden, then dip into melted milk chocolate, about ½ way up, leaving a strip of white chocolate showing. Let harden, then dip tops of berries in melted semisweet chocolate. Store on a wax paper-lined plate in refrigerator.

No Bake Strawberry Dessert

1 (10-ounce) package frozen sliced, sweetened strawberries
2 large egg whites
½ cup sugar
1 tablespoon fresh lemon juice
1 cup whipping cream

Combine partially thawed strawberries, egg whites, sugar, and lemon juice in a large mixing bowl with electric mixer at high speed for 5 minutes or until thick and fluffy. Whip cream, and fold into strawberry mixture. Freeze in molds and serve directly from freezer. Serves 12.

Cheesecake Stuffed Strawberry Bites

These awesome little bites can be made a day ahead.

1 (8-ounce) package cream cheese, softened
1/3 cup powdered sugar
2 teaspoons lemon juice
48 medium strawberries, whole
1/2 cup graham cracker crumbs

Beat together cream cheese, sugar, and lemon juice until creamy; set aside. Using a paring knife, hollow out top of each strawberry, making a shell. Using a pastry bag, fill each just slightly above the tops with cream cheese mixture. Place on cookie sheets. Dip filled strawberries into graham cracker crumbs and place back on cookie sheet. Refrigerate to chill and set. Decorate with mint leaves.

Champagne Sorbet

4 cups water
2 cups sugar
2 cups orange juice
1/2 cup lemon juice
4 cups champagne

Bring water and sugar to a boil; continue cooking until sugar is dissolved. Remove from heat and allow to cool. Once cool, combine with remaining ingredients, and freeze in ice cream maker according to manufacturer's directions.

Refreshing Orange-Pineapple Sherbet

1 (14-ounce) can condensed milk
1 (20-ounce) can crushed pineapple
1 liter orange soda
Ice
Rock salt

Pour milk and pineapple in ice cream freezer container. Stir in half the orange soda, removing the foam with a big spoon. Continue to add soda to the fill line. You probably won't use the whole bottle. Pack container in ice, sprinkle ice with rock salt, and plug in or churn till done. Yummy!

Editor's Extra: Fat-free condensed milk and diet soda can make this a pleasing dessert for all.

Baked Alaska

4 egg whites
¼ teaspoon vanilla
¼ cup sifted confectioners' sugar
1 pint vanilla ice cream
6 mini sponge cakes

Beat egg whites till stiff. Add vanilla, then gradually add confectioners' sugar, beating until stiff peaks form. Divide ice cream equally among each sponge cake. Cover each one completely with egg white mixture. May be made in advance up to this point and frozen.

When ready to serve, place on cookie sheet in 450° oven and quickly brown (takes about 5 minutes). Serves 6.

Coffee Toffee Ice Cream Dessert

28 Oreos, divided
6 (1.4-ounce) Heath or Skor candy bars
½ gallon chocolate ice cream, softened
1 cup chocolate syrup, divided
½ gallon coffee ice cream, softened, divided

Get 3 large zipper bags. Place ½ of Oreos in one bag, and ½ in the other. Place Heath bars in the third bag. Crush each bag with a rolling pin. Sprinkle 1 bag Oreos in bottom of a lightly greased springform pan. Top with chocolate ice cream. Drizzle with ½ the chocolate syrup. Sprinkle with second bag of cookies. Top with coffee ice cream, then drizzle with remaining chocolate syrup. Top with crushed Heath bars. Cover with foil. Freeze until firm.

Peanut Butter Ice Cream Balls

1 cup graham cracker crumbs
2 tablespoons sugar
¼ teaspoon cinnamon
¼ cup peanut butter
1 quart vanilla ice cream

Mix graham cracker crumbs, sugar, and cinnamon. Stir in peanut butter. Form ice cream into large balls, and coat well in crumb mixture. Keep frozen until serving.

Editor's Extra: For added taste, drizzle with chocolate or caramel syrup.

In baseball, the starting point for much of the action on the field is home plate, which is a **five-sided** white rubber slab. Home plate is where play begins, and it is the final base that a player must touch to score.

Home plate began as a twelve-inch square in the 19th century, set down like a diamond, with the two sides forming the beginning of the foul lines. In 1899, the bottom of the plate (the side facing the pitcher) was officially extended, creating the home plate as a **pentagon**. This made it easier for the pitcher to see the width of the plate, and for the umpire to judge balls and strikes with less difficulty.

In baseball, **five** represents the third baseman's position.

Five-Minute Chocolate Trifle

It is absolutely impossible to make an easier, faster, prettier, more delicious dessert.

½ store-bought chocolate cake
½ cup Kahlúa (or strong coffee)
2–3 (4-pack) packages snack-size chocolate pudding
1 (12-ounce) carton frozen whipped topping, thawed
½ (8-ounce) package Heath toffee bits

Break cake into chunks, and layer ½ into a trifle dish. Pour ½ the coffee over this, then ½ of the pudding cups, ½ the whipped topping, then ½ of the toffee bits. Layer again. That's it!

Editor's Extra: You can get chocolate cake at many supermarket bakeries. But if you can't find it, this can be done with pound cake, bought brownies or Twinkies, or even frozen cakes. You can make your own cake and pudding, but it will take a tad longer.

After-Dinner Crème Liqueur

¼ cup Kahlúa
¼ cup amaretto
3 cups vanilla ice cream, softened
1 cup coffee ice cream, softened
¼ cup whipping cream

In large mixing bowl, blend ingredients until smooth. Serve immediately, or freeze until serving time.

Fast
and
Fabulous

FIVE ★ STAR

Extra Help

Equivalents

Apple: 1 medium = 1 cup chopped

Banana: 1 medium = ⅓ cup

Berries: 1 pint = 1¾ cups

Bread: 1 slice = ½ cup soft crumbs = ¼ cup fine, dry crumbs

Broth: 1 cup = 1 bouillon cube dissolved in 1 cup boiling water

Butter: 1 stick = ¼ pound = ½ cup

Cabbage: 2 pounds = 9 cups shredded or 5 cups cooked

Cheese, grated: 1 pound = 4 cups; 8 ounces = 2 cups

Chicken: 1 large boned breast = 2 cups cooked meat

Crabmeat: 1 pound = 3 cups

Chocolate: 1 square or 1 ounce = 2 tablespoons grated

Coconut: 3½-ounce can = 1⅓ cups

Cool Whip: 8 ounces = 3 cups

Crackers, saltine: 23 = 1 cup crushed

Crackers, graham: 15 = 1 cup crushed

Cream, heavy: 1 cup = 2–2½ cups whipped

Egg whites: 8–10 = 1 cup

Eggs: 4–5 = 1 cup

Evaporated milk: 5⅓-ounce can = ⅔ cup; 13-ounce can = 1¼ cups

Flour: 1 pound = 4½ cups

Flour, self-rising: 1 cup = 1 cup all-purpose + 1½ teaspoons baking powder + ½ teaspoon salt

Garlic powder: ⅛ teaspoon = 1 average clove

Herbs, fresh: 1 tablespoon = 1 teaspoon dried

Lemon: 1 medium = 3 tablespoons juice

Marshmallows: ¼ pound = 16 large; ½ cup mini = 4 large

Mushrooms: ¼ pound fresh = 1 cup sliced

Mustard, dry: 1 teaspoon = 1 tablespoon prepared

Noodles: 1 pound = 7 cups cooked

Nuts, chopped: ¼ pound = 1 cup

Onion: 1 medium = ¾–1 cup chopped = 2 tablespoons dried chopped (flakes)

Orange: 3–4 medium = 1 cup juice

Pecans: 1 pound shelled = 4 cups

Potatoes: 1 pound = 3 medium

Rice: 1 cup = 3 cups cooked

Spaghetti: 1 pound uncooked = 5 cups cooked

Spinach, fresh: 2 cups chopped = 1 (10-ounce) package frozen chopped

Sugar, brown: 1 pound = 2½ cups

Sugar, powdered: 1 pound = 3½ cups

Sugar, white: 1 pound = 2¼ cups

Vanilla wafers: 22 = 1 cup fine crumbs

Whole milk: 1 cup = ½ cup evaporated + ½ cup water

Substitutions

1 slice cooked **bacon** = 1 tablespoon bacon bits

1 cup **buttermilk** = 1 cup plain yogurt; or 1 tablespoon lemon
juice or vinegar + plain milk to make 1 cup

1 cup sifted **cake flour** = ⁷⁄₈ cup sifted all-purpose flour

1 ounce **unsweetened chocolate** = 3 tablespoons cocoa +
1 tablespoon butter or margarine

1 ounce **semisweet chocolate** = 3 tablespoons cocoa +
1 tablespoon butter or margarine + 3 tablespoons sugar

1 tablespoon **cornstarch** = 2 tablespoons flour (for thickening)

1 cup **heavy cream** (for cooking, not whipping) = ⅓ cup butter
+ ¾ cup milk

1 cup **sour cream** = ⅓ cup milk + ⅓ cup butter; or 1 cup plain
yogurt

1 cup **tartar sauce** = 6 tablespoons mayonnaise or salad dressing + 2 tablespoons pickle relish

1 cup **tomato juice** = ½ cup tomato sauce + ½ cup water

1 cup **vegetable oil** = ½ pound (2 sticks) butter

1 cup **whipping cream**, whipped = 6–8 ounces Cool Whip

1 cup **whole milk** = ½ cup evaporated milk + ½ cup water

Measurements

3 teaspoons = 1 tablespoon

1 tablespoon = ½ fluid ounce

2 tablespoons = ⅛ cup

3 tablespoons = 1 jigger

4 tablespoons = ¼ cup

8 tablespoons = ½ cup or 4 ounces

12 tablespoons = ¾ cup

16 tablespoons = 1 cup

⅜ cup = ¼ cup + 2 tablespoons

⅝ cup = ½ cup + 2 tablespoons

⅞ cup = ¾ cup + 2 tablespoons

½ cup = 4 fluid ounces

1 cup = ½ pint or 8 fluid ounces

2 cups = 1 pint or 16 fluid ounces

1 pint, liquid = 2 cups or 16 fluid ounces

1 quart, liquid = 2 pints or 4 cups

1 gallon, liquid = 4 quarts or 8 pints or 16 cups

- **Five** tablespoons plus 1 teaspoon equals ⅓ cup.
- One teaspoon equals about **5** milliliters.
- A bale of cotton is about **500** pounds.
- A bolt of fabric is equal to about **50** yards.
- A one-carat diamond is equal to **one-fifth** of a gram.
- Originating in the early 1900s, horse power meant the power needed to lift **550** pounds one foot in one second.
- A knot equals **1.15** miles per hour.
- A magnum is a large bottle equaling **1.5** liters.
- A ream is **500** sheets of paper.
- A **fifth** is a quantity of liquor equal to **one-fifth** of a gallon.

Pan Sizes for Baking

4 cups will fit into
- 8-inch round cake pan
- 9-inch round pie pan
- 9-inch pie pan
- 4x8x2¾-inch loaf pan (small)

5 cups will fit into
- 7x11x1¾-inch pan
- 10-inch pie pan

6 cups will fit into
- 8x8x2-inch square pan
- 5x9x3¼-inch loaf pan (large)

8 cups will fit into
- 9x9x2¼-inch casserole
- 7½x11¾x2-inch pan

12 cups will fit into
- 8½x13½x2½-inch glass dish
- 9x13x2-inch pan

Oven-to-Crockpot

15–30 minutes (oven) = 1½–2½ hours on HIGH or 4–6 hours on LOW

35–45 minutes (oven) = 2–3 hours on HIGH or 6–8 hours on LOW

50 minutes–3 hours (oven) = 4–5 hours on HIGH or 8–10 hours on LOW

Convection Cooking

A convection oven is one that has elements that heat the air, but also a fan that circulates that hot air. This creates more energy, and cooks foods faster and more evenly, giving you crispy exteriors, juicy interiors, and great browning.

Simply reduce the temperature 25° from what your recipe calls for, and expect the foods to be done in less time. For instance, cookies that take eight minutes might be done in six minutes. (Remember to use baking pans with low sides, to take advantage of the convection benefit.)

Fast
and
Fabulous

FIVE ★ STAR

Index

5

BEST OF THE BEST STATE COOKBOOK SERIES

Best of the Best from
ALABAMA
(all-new edition)
(original edition)*

Best of the Best from
ALASKA

Best of the Best from
ARIZONA

Best of the Best from
ARKANSAS

Best of the Best from
BIG SKY
Montana and Wyoming

Best of the Best from
CALIFORNIA

Best of the Best from
COLORADO

Best of the Best from
FLORIDA
(all-new edition)
(original edition)*

Best of the Best from
GEORGIA
(all-new edition)
(original edition)*

Best of the Best from the
GREAT PLAINS
*North and South Dakota,
Nebraska, and Kansas*

Best of the Best from
HAWAI'I

Best of the Best from
IDAHO

Best of the Best from
ILLINOIS

Best of the Best from
INDIANA

Best of the Best from
IOWA

Best of the Best from
KENTUCKY
(all-new edition)
(original edition)*

Best of the Best from
LOUISIANA

Best of the Best from
LOUISIANA II

Best of the Best from
MICHIGAN

Best of the Best from the
MID-ATLANTIC
*Maryland, Delaware, New
Jersey, and Washington, D.C.*

Best of the Best from
MINNESOTA

Best of the Best from
MISSISSIPPI
(all-new edition)
(original edition)*

Best of the Best from
MISSOURI

Best of the Best from
NEVADA

Best of the Best from
NEW ENGLAND
*Rhode Island, Connecticut,
Massachusetts, Vermont,
New Hampshire, and Maine*

Best of the Best from
NEW MEXICO

Best of the Best from
NEW YORK

Best of the Best from
NO. CAROLINA
(all-new edition)
(original edition)*

Best of the Best from
OHIO

Best of the Best from
OKLAHOMA

Best of the Best from
OREGON

Best of the Best from
PENNSYLVANIA

Best of the Best from
SO. CAROLINA
(all-new edition)
(original edition)*

Best of the Best from
TENNESSEE
(all-new edition)
(original edition)*

Best of the Best from
TEXAS

Best of the Best from
TEXAS II

Best of the Best from
UTAH

Best of the Best from
VIRGINIA

Best of the Best from
VIRGINIA II

Best of the Best from
WASHINGTON

Best of the Best from
WEST VIRGINIA

Best of the Best from
WISCONSIN

*Original editions available while supplies last.

*All BEST OF THE BEST STATE COOKBOOKS are 6x9 inches and
comb-bound with illustrations, photographs, and an index.
They range in size from 288 to 352 pages and each contains over 300 recipes.* **Retail price per copy $16.95.**

To order by credit card, call toll-free **1-800-343-1583** or visit **www.quailridge.com.**

Ⓠ Order form

Use this form for sending check or money order to:
QUAIL RIDGE PRESS • P. O. Box 123 • Brandon, MS 39043

❏ Check enclosed

Charge to: ❏ Visa ❏ MC ❏ AmEx ❏ Disc

Card # _____

Expiration Date _____

Signature _____

Name _____

Address_____

City/State/Zip _____

Phone # _____

Email Address _____

Qty.	Title of Book (State) or Set	Total

Subtotal _____

7% Tax for MS residents _____

Postage ($4.00 any number of books) + 4.00

Total _____